Drama and Improvisation

Resource Books for Teachers
series editor Alan Maley

Drama and Improvisation

Ken Wilson

OXFORD
UNIVERSITY PRESS

OXFORD
UNIVERSITY PRESS

Great Clarendon Street, Oxford OX2 6DP

Oxford University Press is a department of the University of Oxford.
It furthers the University's objective of excellence in research, scholarship,
and education by publishing worldwide in

Oxford New York

Auckland Cape Town Dar es Salaam Hong Kong Karachi
Kuala Lumpur Madrid Melbourne Mexico City Nairobi
New Delhi Shanghai Taipei Toronto

With offices in

Argentina Austria Brazil Chile Czech Republic France Greece
Guatemala Hungary Italy Japan Poland Portugal Singapore
South Korea Switzerland Thailand Turkey Ukraine Vietnam

OXFORD and OXFORD ENGLISH are registered trade marks of
Oxford University Press in the UK and in certain other countries

ISBN: 978 0 19 442580 3

Printed in China

Acknowledgements

During the 1990s, my wife Dede and I did a teacher development summer school in the middle of the Hungarian plain at a place called Bugac. The course was called *Drama Plus* and was attended by teachers from more than 30 countries. Many of the ideas in this book were developed with the participants at *Drama Plus*, who then tried them out on their own students when they went home. The information gained from this international exposure to the activities is reflected in the notes relating to the material.

I have also seen inspiring work done by extra-curricular English clubs that teachers with more energy than me have started in schools all over the world. Many of these teachers make drama and performance the focus of such extra English activities. In particular, I want to pay tribute to the students and teachers who attend the annual Teenplay Drama Festival in Arad, Romania, where I was lucky enough to be president of the jury on two occasions. The work done by the teachers and students in those groups is staggeringly good, and Romania is one of the many countries where an interest in English and an interest in drama, theatre, and performance seem to go hand in hand.

My co-directors at the English Teaching Theatre, Hazel Imbert and the late Doug Case, have both had a profound influence on my drama training ideas and written work. Both Hazel and Doug were wonderful working partners, and were instrumental in the development of many of these ideas.

I am also indebted to the many ETT actors whose ideas I have been able to adapt for this book. I have been fortunate to work with some extremely talented and energetic young actors. Apart from anything else, they showed me that good actors are incredibly hard-working and dedicated people.

I want to give a special mention to two of these colleagues: Joy Harrison, an actor-director with amazing energy and an endless fund of good ideas, who has accompanied Dede and me on various ELT drama training ventures; and Richard Vranch, who was a member of both the English Teaching Theatre and the Comedy Store Players and who introduced me to the work of the Players.

The Comedy Store Players

The Comedy Store Players are a group of improvising comedy performers who are based at the Comedy Store in London. The group began in 1985, and the original line-up included Mike Myers, who was later to become internationally famous as the parody spy in the *Austin Powers* series of movies. Canadian Myers and an American woman comedian and actor called Kit Hollerbach brought North American improvisation ideas and taught them to an eager group of English actor/comedians.

Viola Spolin (1906–1994)

Many of the Comedy Store improvisations were inspired by the work of educator and actor-director Viola Spolin, the inventor of Theater Games.

Viola Spolin was born in Chicago and initially trained as a settlement worker, someone who helps immigrants to adapt to their new surroundings in the USA. She was aware that language communication was vital to these new Americans, and she was influenced by innovative teaching methods aimed at making groups work well together. She also found ways to use these methods to help individuals in the group feel confident enough to express their feelings.

Spolin was also interested in the way in which game structures affected the social behaviour of inner-city and immigrant children. She was particularly fascinated by the fact that children who were reluctant and resistant to normal teaching methods reacted with enthusiasm and energy if something was introduced as a game. When the children weren't being asked to 'learn' something, they actually learned a lot!

In 1939, while serving as a drama supervisor in Chicago, Spolin began to devise a system of theatre training that could cross cultural and ethnic barriers. She began to develop new games that focused on individual creativity, using the concept of play to unlock the individual's creativity and self-expression. These techniques were later to be formalized under the title *Theater Games*. She said, 'The games emerged out of necessity. I didn't sit at home and dream them up. When I had a problem with the children, I made up a game. When another problem came up, I just made up a new game.'

Her son Paul Sills developed the comic potential of these games, and opened Second City, the first improvisation comedy club in the world, in Chicago. When they opened a new club in Montreal, Canada, one of the first people to attend the show was Mike Myers, then aged 14.

Dedication

This book is dedicated to the memory of two people: Doug Case, my life-long working partner and friend, without whose influence and advice this book would never have been written; and my lovely sister-in-law Lesley Wilson. Both sorely missed.

Contents

	Activity	Level	Time (minutes)	Aims	

5 Working with scripts

The author and series editor

Ken Wilson is an ELT materials author whose work also involves training, theatre, music, audio production, and writing for radio and TV. He has written ten series of coursebooks and vast amounts of supplementary material, including books of sketches and more than 150 ELT songs. His course material includes *Smart Choice*, a four-level course for young adult learners, also published by OUP.

Ken has trained teachers all over Europe, Latin America, and Asia. After working as a CELTA trainer, he began to develop drama techniques and incorporate them into more conventional teaching methods. With his wife Dede, he ran a summer school called 'Drama Plus' for ten years in Hungary. Teachers from 30 countries attended these courses. More recently, he has trained teachers in China and other Asian countries.

After his first teaching job in Seville, Ken moved to International House, London, where he became a teacher trainer. In his free time, he started playing in a band, which led directly to two new strands of his working life. Firstly, he wrote songs for his English students, which resulted in the recording of the first-ever album of ELT songs, *Mister Monday*. Secondly, he joined the English Teaching Theatre (ETT) as a teacher/musician. He eventually became artistic director of the company.

The English Teaching Theatre was the brainchild of John Haycraft, the founder of the International House chain of language schools. Over a period of 25 years, the ETT made more than 250 tours to 55 countries. The actors who worked at the ETT, and the teachers and students that Ken met in these countries have been a major source of inspiration for the ideas in this book.

Alan Maley worked for the British Council from 1966 to 1988, serving as English Language Officer in Yugoslavia, Ghana, Italy, France, and China, and as Regional Representative in South India (Madras). From 1988 to 1993, he was Director-General of the Bell Educational Trust, Cambridge. From 1993 to 1998 he was Senior Fellow in the Department of English Language and Literature of the National University of Singapore, and from 1998 to 2003 he was Director of the graduate programme at Assumption University, Bangkok. He is currently a freelance consultant. Among his publications are *Literature* (in this series), *Beyond Words*, *Sounds Interesting*, *Sounds Intriguing*, *Words*, *Variations on a Theme*, and *Drama*

Techniques in Language Learning (all with Alan Duff), *The Mind's Eye* (with Françoise Grellet and Alan Duff), *Learning to Listen* and *Poem into Poem* (with Sandra Moulding), *Short and Sweet*, and *The English Teacher's Voice*.

Foreword

Despite all the innovations which have entered the language teaching profession in the wake of the 'communicative revolution', it remains true that the vast majority of what happens in classrooms is highly structured and controlled. It tends to be focused on supposedly predictable outcomes to be achieved by concentrated, effortful activities, which can be measured in tests and examinations.

There is, however, abundant evidence that languages are not learned or acquired only in this way. There is an important role for activities which focus on playfulness, on enjoyment, on physical movement, on affective engagement, and which can foster what has been called a 'flow' state of effortless effort.

There is, of course, no single way of achieving 'flow' but using drama and improvisation is one of the well-attested ways of moving towards it. They build confidence and an ability to handle the very unpredictability which lies at the heart of interactions in the new language. They foster the capacity to deal imaginatively with the unexpected, and the willingness to 'have a go'—to take risks in the new language. In the absence of this capability, little enduring learning is likely to take place.

The activities in this book are designed specifically to help learners loosen up, to engage creatively with the new language in a context of support and cooperative effort. This is not a course book, yet the chapters do tend to lead from shorter, simpler, less demanding activities towards longer and more complex activities, culminating in a series of ideas for working with a series of original dramatic sketches in English.

The author has distilled his experience of working with teachers and students, and with the actors of the English Teaching Theatre and their audiences, over many years in many different geographical and educational contexts. The activities themselves bear the stamp of authentic experience and proven success. This book is a breath of fresh air and will prove a welcome new bank of activities for the resourceful teacher!

Alan Maley

Introduction

Why was this book written?

Drama and Improvisation is a series of activities designed to enliven your English classes and activate your students' imagination and creativity. I devised and collected them over many years working as a language trainer and actor/director with the English Teaching Theatre (ETT). Many of them emerged from improvisation activities with students in class or with teachers at workshops and on courses all over the world. Some of them were inspired by working with ETT actors and some are adaptations of material used by a London-based group of improvisation actors and comedians called the Comedy Store Players.

There is much more in this book than is usually covered by the word 'drama'. There are activities whose main purpose is to energize a class, to make the students feel positive and ready to work. Other activities are designed to encourage student creativity, sometimes simple, sometimes complex, but always exciting for the student. There is also material for use with an extra-curricular English drama club and eight original sketches.

How do these activities help the teacher?

I'm sure that teachers who enjoy using drama activities in class and regularly use them will find a lot of interesting new material in this book. However, I'm also interested in providing manageable material for teachers who have less experience of using such activities or who think that they do not have time for them.

Most teachers have very little time to do anything in the class apart from following the coursebook and preparing for exams or tests. Following the dictates of a coursebook and the requirements of an exam often mean that teachers become lecturers and providers of information, which can mean that students spend a lot of time only passively involved with the lesson. This situation can be improved by an activity that inspires students in a way that 'normal' class activities do not. This book is full of such activities.

Most of the activities in this book are quick to set up, fun to do, and do not take up much of the lesson. They will wake the students up and make them ready for the next compulsory and possibly passive part of the lesson.

They also provide you with the chance to relinquish some responsibility for class management, in effect to take a well-earned breather. There are, of course, times when you have to be in charge, for example when you are teaching a new grammar item. However, there are also times when you can make the students responsible for what happens. Most students thrive on this responsibility. The notes accompanying the activities have recommendations of how and when to make the students responsible for classroom management.

How do these activities help the learner?

There are learners who love their teachers but still find English classes an ordeal. Many of them find the academic side of the learning process not to their taste. They do not respond well to a diet of mainly grammar practice and skills work, and their energy and motivation leak away at certain points of the lesson. Worst of all, they feel that they are a disappointment to the teacher. However, these same students have skills which lie dormant. They may do any number of things well—act, sing, mime, draw—and they may be very quick-witted.

It would be impossible and in any case inappropriate for you to re-model your methodology entirely to make these students happy. However, if you can find time to include an activity from this book at some point, it will give you a golden opportunity to connect with the students who do not respond to regular classroom activities.

What are the advantages of these techniques?

The majority of activities in this book are for teachers who want to enliven their classes and refresh students who may be tired or subdued by the way they are asked to learn. The classroom activities are short, easy to do, and success-oriented; in other words, it is easy for the students to get them right. They are designed so as not to make the students feel inadequate or frustrated even if their communicative ability is limited.

They are also designed to access the creative talents of your students, and to give them the chance to say or write simple but unique things. They also offer more responsibility to the students themselves to make things happen in the classroom because you do not have to be the only one giving instructions or leading and developing classroom activities.

The activities in Chapter 4 are designed to be used in extra-curricular drama clubs. The drama club activities take a little longer to set up, but are enjoyable, rewarding, and give participants a wonderful sense of achievement.

How to use this book

What does each activity contain?

At the beginning of each activity, there are three pieces of information: the level the activity is aimed at, the time it should take, and the aims. It looks like this:

Level   Elementary +

Time   15 minutes

Aims   To help students learn and remember each other's names.

The level of more than half of the activities is Elementary +. In fact, this means that they are useful to teachers of all levels, up to and including Advanced. I hope that teachers of all levels will read the activities marked Elementary +, and see the possibilities of using them with their classes, regardless of level.

There are three other sections in the notes accompanying each activity. They are entitled *Preparation*, *Procedure* and *Follow-up*.

Preparation lists the things that need doing before an activity. You may be pleased to note that in many cases, the instruction is that no preparation at all is needed! *Procedure* lists the way the activity can be carried out, and *Follow-up* gives a suggestion for something that can be done after the activity. In many cases, the activity is enough of a challenge for the students, and teachers may prefer to go back to their normal book-based lesson immediately after completing it.

I want to emphasize at this point that procedure notes do NOT constitute hard and fast rules. They simply offer ONE way to do the activity, not the only way.

After this, there are two occasional sections: *Variation* and *Comments*. *Variation* lists alternative ways that the activity might work. The *Comments* section adds thoughts based on experience of doing the activities and sometimes lists the pitfalls and dangers. These may be from my personal experience, or they may represent a note that was given to me by teachers who tried the activity with their students after attending one of my courses or workshops.

How is the book organized?

Chapter 1 Hello and welcome!

These are activities for a new class and are designed to make the first lessons amusing and memorable, but the actual language requirement for most of them is quite low and manageable. They are also designed to help students who feel a little nervous or apprehensive at the start of a new course. The activities emphasize the social bonding of the class, rather than language development.

Chapter 2 Classroom interaction and improvisation

This chapter contains classroom activities which are designed to encourage students to interact with each other and to improvise. The activities are short and manageable enough to be done without causing too much disruption. The level of creativity and imagination which is involved is actually very easy to achieve.

Chapter 3 Fun and games

The activities in this section are all fun activities and most involve some kind of movement. They are perfect to break up a lesson where students would otherwise sit at their desks for an hour or longer. They are quite short and will definitely improve the overall atmosphere of the class.

Chapter 4 Drama club

These activities are designed for teachers who want to organize an extra-curricular activity which involves English. The first seven activities are warm-up activities, some of them quite physical, and many of them requiring little English, so they should be manageable with a group of enthusiastic but mixed ability students. The remaining eight activities require greater ability with English, as the students are encouraged to improvise and 'think on their feet'. All the activities can also be used in a normal class, if you think you have the time and the right space for them.

Chapter 5 Working with scripts

'Scripts' refers to any long dialogue, sketch, or short play that you might want to use with your class or drama group. This chapter contains a set of eight original sketches and eight suggestions about how to use them. Each of the sketches is used to illustrate a different activity, but in fact the activities are interchangeable, and most of them will work with any short dramatic piece that you want to use.

Notes for teachers

Warmers

I don't normally use the word 'warmers' because I think that, with most classes, the beginning of the lesson is not necessarily the best time for the activities in this book, whether you are teaching teenagers or adults. Most teenage students I have met need to be calmed down rather than warmed up at the beginning of a class and adult students want to get down to work when they arrive, and may feel a little frustrated if they have to do a warmer/mingler first. Also, as one teacher said to me: 'I don't use warmers because my students trickle in.' The activities in this book are best used in the middle of a class, when attention levels and energy are failing.

There are two exceptions. The activities in Chapter 1 are designed for new classes, and could be called ice-breakers. In Chapter 4, the activities are designed for use in an extra-curricular drama club, so the first seven activities are designed as warm-up activities. Many of them require little English, so they should be manageable with a group of enthusiastic but mixed ability students. Apart from their warm-up value, they are also designed to help the students realize that this is not a normal English class, and the usual classroom rules and relationships need not apply, though they may also be used as classroom activities.

Teacher control

There are activities in this book where the teacher has to relinquish control of events. I think this is a good thing for all kinds of reasons, not least because teaching is tiring and we all need a break. Some activities, such as 2.3 *Be someone else*, are designed so that the students take over the management of the event once you have set it up.

You need to be in control most of the time. You are the captain of the ship. But there are times when it is good for you to give control to the crew. They may teach you something!

Error correction

You will of course hear lots of errors during the freer activities. Most methodology experts recommend that you should not stop a successful drama activity to correct someone's English. It does help, however, if you can make a mental note of something you want to correct later. However, it is your class and your rules apply, so if you normally stop activities when you hear errors, then you should continue to do this.

There are, however, two main advantages of waiting until later before correcting mistakes that you hear. Firstly, there is no need to name the student or students who made the mistakes, thus avoiding any embarrassment; secondly, if the activity was funny or memorable in other ways, the students will enjoy being reminded of what happened.

Student suspicion

There are several activities in this book where you ask students a question and the answer is something that they have to imagine for themselves, but which in a 'normal' lesson they might not expect to be answering. A good example is Activity 2.2 *Gifted athletes*. Part of the build-up to this activity involves the students telling you where the conference for gifted athletes is taking place.

When you first try an activity like this, students may be a little confused or even suspicious. This is because many students seem to think that when teachers ask questions, they always have a particular answer in mind. Some students don't recognize the difference between the following three questions:

- What is the past tense of 'give'?
- What is the capital of Peru?
- What do you think the man in the picture does for a living?

The basic problem is that almost all students react badly to the 'n' word: *No*. And the 'w' word: *wrong*. And the worst thing for them is when they hear the two words in the same sentence: *No, that's wrong*.

With activities like *Gifted athletes*, it may take a little time for them to realize that you really do not have an answer to the question you are asking, and you really do want them to provide some background information. For this reason, *Gifted athletes* is one of the most important activities in the book, and I recommend that you do it with every new class you take.

Students who are not 'good at English'

We tend to think of our students as 'good at English' or 'not good at English'. Apart from that, we may like them as individuals, but we may know little about their non-academic abilities and talents. With the activities in this book, students who are not good at English can shine—perhaps because they are good at mime, or they are athletic or quick-witted.

Shy and quiet students

When I do these activities at conferences or on training courses, I always ask teachers to send me any comments if they try them out with their students. I always emphasize that I want feedback, whether positive or negative. One of the negative comments I often hear is that shy and quiet students 'don't get involved'.

There are drama experts who will tell you that drama activities are the best way to make shy students throw off their cloak of shyness and take centre stage, and to make quiet students suddenly become the star of the show. It is possible that this might happen but I think it is unlikely. I see the situation rather differently. I think that shy and quiet students can enjoy these activities even if they do not get actively involved.

For example, in Activity 2.11 *Who's that?*, students work in groups first, inventing personas for students in other groups. They then interview them. If the interviewer says that the interviewee is a pop star, the interviewee has to accept that and answer questions about being a pop star.

In reality, in an average class of teenagers or adults, there are only a handful of people that students want to interview. Let's call them the A-list. Similarly, being an interviewer will appeal to some students more than others. Let's call them the B-list. Finally, there are students who will be neither interesting enough to interview nor engaged enough to become an interviewer. Let's call them the C-list. C-listers will usually be shy and/or quiet students, and there is not much you the teacher can do about this. However, having C-list students in your class doesn't mean you can't do the activities. In my experience, they enjoy watching and listening to activities where A- and B-listers are doing something creative and amusing.

Students who talk too much

This is of course connected to the above note. When students overcome their worries about providing input, some of them talk too much. This talk is not always useful to the activity. In Activity 2.12 *Fishbowl*, for example, where students have to shout the word *Fish!* to move the activity on, some students shout it too often. Discourage this; try to get more and more students involved, especially in activities like this one where the required student response is easy.

Self-regulating improvisations

The good thing about many of the activities in this book is that they are self-regulating. What I mean by this is that the activity works at the level of the students, whether they are elementary or advanced. Take Activity 2.3 *Be someone else*, for example. A student (Student A) answers four simple questions in order to adopt a completely new persona. The rest of the class ask him or her questions. Obviously, they only ask questions that they are able to ask. If someone asks a question which is too difficult for Student A to answer, the students will work it out for themselves. In a monolingual class, typically, Student A will ask for a translation of the question.

Unreal activities

Some teachers say they feel a bit strange asking students to talk about things which are unreal or impossible. This was a comment I had about Activity 2.5 *Hobbies and locations*. Whilst I can understand the teacher's fears that the students are using language which they will not use in everyday life, this is certainly not a problem for the students themselves. In fact, it is the very juxtaposition of strange events which makes these activities so memorable.

Incentives to listen

An added bonus of many activities in this book is that while certain students are saying something, the rest of the class really want to listen. How often does that happen?

Accept and add

Accept and Add is a central tenet of improvisation theatre. I do not expect students to become familiar with this or any other theory of acting, but this particular one is important for some of the activities in this book. What it means is that if someone says something to you in an improvised scene, you have to accept what they say as the reality of the situation and add to it. Improvised activities break down if this convention is not followed. For example: in Activity 2.11 *Who's that?*, students invent personas for other people in the room and then interview them. Let's imagine that Student A decides that Student B is a novelist. Student A starts the interview by saying: *What is your latest novel about?* If Student B answers: *I'm not a novelist, I'm a taxi-driver*, this can be amusing, but it wrecks the activity.

You don't need to tell your students anything about this drama theory. All you need to do at the beginning of an activity like this one is say: *Whatever people say to you, accept it—don't change it.*

Positive feedback

Positive feedback is tremendously important, especially in a drama club session, where the students are not there just to improve the accuracy of their English. Even if your initial thought is to correct an error immediately, try not to do it. Instead, congratulate participants on their imagination, quick-wittedness, or humour. There will be plenty of opportunities to do correction later.

Stand-by class

Stand-by classes are the classes that you have to take which are not your own, because the usual teacher is unavailable for some reason. I recommend putting together three or four of these activities to make the perfect stand-by class lesson plan.

Laughter

Students learn and then quickly forget most things that they are taught. The main problem of teaching is getting them to remember new material—structures or vocabulary—for days, hours, even minutes after it has been first presented and practised. Laughter is the best *aide-memoire* a teacher could ask for. If you let your students free with some of these activities, there will be laughter and occasionally a little mayhem. I think both of these things are beneficial, occasionally, in the classroom.

Offensive language

This is a particular problem where the activity requires the students to write things down which are then read aloud by other people. Activity 2.4 *Actions and locations* is a good example. Students write actions and locations on pieces of paper, which are then put into boxes, to be read later by other students acting out a scene. The activity provides an opportunity for a certain kind of student to write something offensive.

My only answer to this is to appeal to their better judgement before the activity starts: point out that writing offensive things is extremely childish and will not be fun for their classmates who have to read them. To make sure that no offensive words are read out, tell participants to ignore anything they read which they do not like.

Fortunately, most of us will not have to experience this problem.

1

Hello and welcome!

These are activities for a new class. Most teachers have successful ways of dealing with a new group of students, and these are not intended to replace your tried and tested routines. However, you may find some ideas here to augment and accompany what you already do.

The activities are designed to make the first lessons amusing and memorable, but the actual language requirement for most of them is quite low and manageable. Whatever the supposed level of a new class, we should always remember that some students may not be at their articulate best immediately.

Many students feel a little nervous or apprehensive at the start of a new course. Even a sympathetic smile from the teacher cannot completely remove this fear. This is why the activities in this chapter emphasize the social bonding of the class, rather than language development.

It is important for students to make an effort to know each other's names, so a lot of the activities are designed to help students do this in a fun way. You can use some of these activities with classes who theoretically already know each other but who have not yet learnt all the names of the other students.

Some of the activities in this section are variations on a theme, so it is not advisable to try them all with the same class. However, if the class still find it difficult to remember each other's names, then maybe you can return to these activities in the second or subsequent weeks of the term/course.

Activity 1.6 will also help you find out what your students already know about the topics covered in your coursebook. There will probably be people in your class who know more about sport, music, and/or movies than you do, and they may even know about mathematics, science, history, and other school subjects as well, the kind of thing that language professionals may know nothing about. It will help you to know what your students already know, so that you can exploit it at some stage during the course.

Activities 1.7 and 1.10 are designed for a class where the teacher is new but the students all know each other.

1.1 Hello, Anna! (Wrong name introductions)

Level Elementary +

Time 15 minutes

Aims To introduce students to each other and help them remember each other's names.

Preparation

No preparation is needed, but this is a mingler activity, and it would help to put all the desks and chairs against the wall of the room. It only takes two or three minutes to do that!

Procedure

1 Put the class in a group in the middle of the room. Tell them that they are going to walk round the room and say *Hello!* to everyone else and address them by name. But as they have not learnt each other's names yet, they will probably address each other by the wrong name. The person they speak to will address them by the wrong name, too. The aim is that both students will then politely correct each other.

2 First of all, elicit things that you can say when you make a mistake about someone's name. Remind the students that you want the exchange to be polite. With the help of the class, write a basic dialogue on the board.

Example *Student A: Hello, Anna!*
Student B: Hello, Adam!
Student A: Actually, my name isn't Adam.
Student B: Isn't it? Sorry!
Student A: That's all right.
Student B: My name isn't Anna, either.
Student A: Oh no! Sorry!
Student B: That's all right.
Student A: What IS your name?
Student B: Magda. And yours?
Student A: Tomas.
Student B: OK! Hello, Tomas. Nice to meet you.
Student A: Nice to meet you, too, Anna.

3 This skeleton may seem long, but it is simple and is a template that can be varied. Students can achieve the same result with other words and expressions. Encourage them to accept and return the greeting before they correct the name. Explain that the following would be considered impolite by most native English speakers:

Student A: Hello, Anna!
Student B: No, I'm not Anna.

4 Students mingle for a few minutes, and try to talk to everyone in the class. As they mingle, they may find themselves talking to people they have already spoken to. If they can remember the name

of the student they have already spoken to, they can address them
by their real name. If they can't remember, then they can repeat the
'wrong name introduction' procedure.

Follow-up

Ask students to come to the front of the class in pairs or threes to tell
you the names of all the other students. This is so that they can help
each other, and no student feels embarrassed about not being able to
remember a particular name. By the end of this activity, students will
have engaged with each other in a positive and energetic way.

Comments

1 I always recommend that students have an alphabetical and
   international list of men's and women's names in their mind as
   they mingle, and they use the names in alphabetical order: for
   example Anna/Adam, Betty/Ben, Carla/Charlie, Donna/Dietrich,
   Erica/Eddie, Fernando/Fiona, etc. They can then go through their
   personal alphabet of names as they meet different people.

2 You will notice that I recommend the use of polite forms and using
   the word *Sorry* when things go wrong, in this and later activities. It
   is worth telling the class that native English speakers, particularly
   from Britain, say *Sorry* more than many other nationalities. It is said
   out of habit and politeness rather than a genuine sense of being
   apologetic. American English speakers say *Excuse me* more than *Sorry*.

3 This is actually a good activity to do with a class who have been
   together for a while. It is much less embarrassing to learn names
   this way than to continue studying in the same room as a group of
   people whose names you don't know.

1.2 Alphabetical order

Level Elementary +

Time 15 minutes

Aims To help students learn each other's names (and nationalities) by
trial and error.

Preparation

No preparation is needed, but this activity works best if the students
are standing in a circle. If this is impossible, then they should stand
around the walls of the classroom.

Procedure

1 Tell the class to form a circle in alphabetical order of their first
   names. Let them do it by themselves rather than managing it for
   them. If you like, you can stand in the circle, too. Tell people to
   introduce themselves to the people on either side of them.

2 In a monolingual class, tell the students that they are going to try to guess the names of other students in the circle from the first letter of the name. Demonstrate what you want by addressing another member of the circle.

Example *Teacher: Excuse me?*
Student A: Yes?
Teacher: Can you tell me the first letter of your name?
Student A: C
Teacher: Is your name Carla?
Student A: No, it isn't.
Teacher: Oh, sorry.
Student A: That's all right.

You then invite another student to try to guess the name.

Example *Student B: Is your name Cristina?*
Student A: No.
Student B: Oh, sorry.
Student A: That's all right.
Student C: Is your name Carolina?
Student A: No …

Keep inviting more students to guess the name until they get it. If they have not guessed after five attempts, say *We give up!* You then ask one of the students on either side of Student A to tell the rest of the class what his/her name is. The chances are they will have forgotten in the few minutes since they introduced themselves, so they will have to apologize and ask for it again.

Example *Student D: I'm really sorry, I've forgotten your name.*
Student A: That's all right. My name is Claire.

3 With a multilingual/multinational group, students can first ask for the nationality of the student they are addressing. They can then make a guess based on names that people of that nationality have. If they don't know any typical names, they should apologize and invite someone else to help them.

You can demonstrate it as follows:

Example *Teacher: Excuse me?*
Student A: Yes?
Teacher: Can you tell me where you are from?
Student A: I'm from Italy.
Teacher: Can you tell me the first letter of your name?
Student A: C
Teacher: Is your name Carla?
Student A: No, it isn't.
Teacher: Oh, sorry.
Student A: That's all right.

or

Teacher: Oh dear … I don't know any Italian girls' names. Can anyone help me?

If there is a student in the class from a country which the rest of the class are unfamiliar with, ask him/her to say what his/her name is and encourage students to ask questions about the name.

Example   *Teacher: I'm sorry. We don't know any names from your country.*
       What's your name?
Student A: Amalie.
Teacher: That's a nice name. What does it mean?
Student A: It means 'hope'.
Student B: Is it a common name in your country?
Student A: Yes, it is.
Student C: Can you tell us some other names from your country?

Follow-up

As with Activity 1.1, you can ask students to come to the front of the class in pairs or threes and remember as many names as they can.

Comments

See the Comment at Activity 1.1 about *Sorry*.

1.3 Birthday connections

Level   Elementary +

Time   15 minutes

Aims   To connect students' birthdays with other events. To practise ordinal numbers and dates.

Preparation

Students need to be able to say dates in English. You may need to pre-teach or revise ordinal numbers and word order of dates before you start. Again, this activity works better if students are standing in a circle.

Procedure

1   Tell students to get in a circle according to their birthdays. Let them do it by themselves rather than managing it for them. If you like, you can stand in the circle, too.

2   Tell the class that you want them to find out when other students' birthdays are. They start by asking for each other's names (if it is not the first day of the course, they should apologize if they don't know them). If students seem to be familiar with the names of their classmates, tell them to address each other by name first and then ask about their birthdays.

Example   *Teacher: Carla?*
Student A: Yes?
Teacher: When is your birthday?
Student A: The fourteenth of June.

3   When the student says her birthday, ask the rest of the class to make a connection with it. Demonstrate what you want by giving an example yourself.

Example *Teacher: The fourteenth of June? That's one week before my sister's birthday.*

Students may take a little time to get used to this idea, but encourage them to make connections, even if the connection is months apart— *That's three months before my parents' wedding anniversary.* Encourage them to think of festivals or other days of national importance in their own countries as well. Here are some other useful expressions:

It's (almost) the same day as …
It's the day before/after …
It's a week/two weeks before/after …

Follow-up

Students should write a paragraph for homework, connecting the birthdays of other students with people, events, or celebrations that they can relate to.

Comments

1 This is a particularly good bonding activity with multinational classes. It is interesting for a student to discover that his/her birthday is, for example, the national day in the country where another student comes from.

2 If you have a multinational class, and students come from countries which have been in conflict with each other, it may be best to avoid this activity. A student of mine connected all the other birthdays to important dates in a conflict between his country and the country of another student.

1.4 Flowing introductions

Level Elementary +

Time 15–30 minutes

Aims To allow students to exchange information with each other.

Preparation

Students will begin in pairs, then form groups of four, and finally they will be in four groups. In other words, if there are twenty students in the class, there will be five students in each of the final groups. They need a pen/pencil and notebook. You need some pieces of paper with the letters A, B, C, and D on them.

Procedure

1 Put the students in pairs. Ask them to write down four things about their partner: their name, plus three other pieces of personal information. Tell them not to ask about family or work/study. Tell them to make a note of all four pieces of information. Give them examples of other things they can ask about.

Examples *What's your favourite colour/kind of music?*
What's your favourite place in your country?

1.7 Our new teacher

Level Elementary +

Time 15 minutes

Aims To help you find out about a new class of students who all know each other.

Preparation

No preparation is required for this activity. If the school requires you to take a register or do other preliminary work with the students before anything else happens, then the following procedure can start as soon as that is finished. If there are no preliminary requirements (or if they can be done later), you can start the moment you walk into the room for the first time.

Procedure

Although this is an activity for a class who all know each other, it may also be used with a class who almost all know each other (see procedure note 6 below). The following procedure presumes that any required preliminary work—taking registers, checking receipts etc.—has been completed.

1 If it is normal for a class to stand up when a teacher enters the room, thank them and ask them to sit down.

2 Introduce yourself as the new teacher. Give as much or as little information about yourself as you wish. (See Comment.)

3 Look around the class and find the most confident-looking student (Student A). Introduce yourself to him/her. Decide if you want to be formal or informal in this introduction. If you have a class of teenagers, you may find that informal works better.

Example *Teacher: Hello, my name is Joan/My name is Ms Watson. What's your name?*
Student A: Dolores.
Teacher: How do you do, Dolores?/Nice to meet you, Dolores.
Student A: How do you do?/Nice to meet you, too.

If the student gets a little tongue-tied during this exchange, invite other students to complete the conversation for him/her. It is always easier when you are not the one in the spotlight!

4 Now indicate another student, Student B, and ask Student A to introduce you to him/her. Student B should preferably be on the other side of the room. Ask Student A to stand up and accompany you to where Student B is sitting. Student B will probably stand up out of politeness. This is good. It makes the introduction feel more natural if all three of you are standing up. Ask Student A to introduce you to Student B.

Example   *Student A: Maria, I'd like you to meet Joan/Ms Watson. She's our new teacher.*
Student B: How do you do, Ms Watson?/Nice to meet you, Joan.
Teacher: How do you do?/Nice to meet you, too, Maria.

5   Thank Student A and tell Student B that you would like him/her to introduce you to someone else. Indicate the next student that you want to meet. Again, it is better to choose someone who is on the other side of the room. Walk across the room with Student B and ask him/her to introduce you to Student C.

6   If there are some new students in the class, you have a choice how to deal with this. You could ask who is new before you start the activity, so you know where the new students are. However, if you do this they may think they have to stand up and say something about themselves, and it may make them nervous. It will naturally become clear which are the new students, and you and the students can deal with it. Here is an example of what might happen.

Example   *Teacher: Maria, can you introduce me to that young man over there?*
Student B: He's new. I don't know his name.
Teacher: OK, let's meet him together. Hello, I'm Joan. What's your name?
Student C: Eric.
Teacher: Nice to meet you, Eric.
Student C: Nice to meet you, too, Joan.
Teacher: I'd like you to meet Maria. Maria, this is Eric.
Student B: Nice to meet you, Eric.
Student C: Nice to meet you, Maria.

Don't worry that the rest of the class have nothing to do. This ambulatory activity is great to watch, and of course the whole class will be involved at some point.

Follow-up

Ask students to come to the front of the class in pairs or threes and remember as many names as they can. This way, they can help each other, and no student feels embarrassed about not being able to remember.

Comments

The question of how much or how little information teachers give about themselves depends a lot on the institution that they work in. It is not normal for state school teachers in most countries to say anything about themselves at all. On the other hand, native-speaker teachers (NESTs) who work in Private Language Schools (PLS) or who work as assistants to non-NESTs in state schools and colleges often like to talk about themselves and where they are from. Remember that you may be the first NEST that the class have ever seen 'in the flesh'.

Example   B: *I'm the kind of person who likes meeting people.*
A: *Really? What do you mean? In real life? In an Internet chatroom?*
B: *I'm the kind of person who is keen on sport.*
A: *Me too! I'm a big football fan. Do you like football?*

Time the minute and tell them to stop when it ends.

5   Student As now repeat the information. Student Bs can react and respond, interrupting if necessary to add or correct information.

Example   A: *You're the kind of person who likes meeting people, but not in chatrooms.*
B: *Well, that isn't exactly what I said. I said chatrooms aren't my favourite place to meet people.*

Follow-up

Discuss with the students how they felt about this activity. How did Student Bs feel about having to be impassive when Student As were talking? Was it hard? Or did they find it enjoyable not to have to respond? Some students find it very restful. However, you may find that Student Bs react badly to being interrupted, especially after having to listen impassively themselves.

Comments

In my experience, discussion of this activity reveals that some female students feel that some male students tend not only to dominate certain parts of the class (discussions, group work, etc.), but to interrupt when female students are speaking or contributing in some other way. I call this kind of classroom interruption 'hi-jacking'. As a result of this, I try to put the students into male–female pairings, and to make the male students Student Bs.

1.10   Find someone who ...

Level   Intermediate +

Time   15 minutes

Aims   To help you find out about a new class of students who all know each other.

Find someone who... worksheets usually require students to mingle with other students, finding someone with red hair, pink socks, etc. This activity reverses the procedure. Here it is the teacher who has to mingle and find particular people.

Preparation

The only requirement is that all the students know each other. Only the teacher is new. Activity 1.9 is possible with a class with some new students, but this activity is difficult if the class do not all know each other.

Procedure

1 Put the class into groups of four or five and tell them to think of something that is unique about each one of them. Tell them not to choose things which are visible, such as long hair, red hair, or blue eyes. Help them by writing some examples on the board.

Examples   *I've visited Disneyland.*
My uncle lives in California.
I've got fifteen cousins.

Ask them to confer with other people in the group to get some ideas and then write a sentence about themselves. Hopefully, they will choose something which is completely unique, but it is possible that they will choose something which they share with someone else in the class. This will come out in the next stage and is not a problem.

2 Tell a representative from each group to collect the papers and confer with representatives from other groups. They should quickly check through the papers to make sure there aren't too many that contain the same or similar information. They then give you the pile of papers.

3 You read the papers and look around the room. It is not likely that you can match the sentences easily with the people, but you can give the impression that you are trying.

4 Walk to a student and ask a question based on the first piece of paper.

Example   *Have you visited Disneyland?*

It is more than likely that the first student will answer *No.* Ask the question a maximum of three times and then ask: *OK … who's been to Disneyland?* When the student who has been to Disneyland indicates who he/she is, give the piece of paper back to him/her and ask for his/her name. If more than one student puts up their hand, check through the papers and give the other one(s) back as well.

5 Important! As you give the paper(s) back, tell the class to make a note of the information that they hear. They already know each other's names so this should not be a problem for them. If they can't remember someone's name, they can check before the next part of the activity.

6 When you have given the pieces of paper back to all the students, ask the class to remind you who has done what. Students read from their notes and tell you.

Examples *Eric has been to Disneyland.*
Marcia's uncle lives in California.
Tomas has fifteen cousins.

Follow-up

Students write an essay: 'What I discovered about my classmates today'.

Comments

1 This activity is set at Intermediate + as students need to know the present perfect for achievements: *I've been to America*, etc.

2 The problem with the regular *Find someone who* ... Resource Book activity is that it has to be filled with lowest common denominator examples. The advantage of this activity is that every piece of information is real, and some of it may be really interesting and unusual.

2
Classroom interaction and improvisation

This chapter contains classroom activities which are designed to encourage students to interact with each other and to improvise. There are similar activities in Chapter 4 which are more ambitious and time-consuming, and which are designed to be done in an extra-curricular setting such as a drama club.

The activities are short and manageable enough to be done in class, without causing too much disruption. There are listening, speaking, and writing activities. Students will be able to use their imagination, often improvising. As you will see when you read the instructions, the level of creativity and imagination which is involved is actually very easy to achieve.

Very little preparation time is required and the activities are easy to set up. In some cases it is better not to give students any preparation time at all, because this can stifle creativity. The language required to carry out these improvisation tasks is not difficult, and the students will not be frustrated by trying to say something that is beyond their ability.

Many of the activities involve students speaking in front of the class, usually as part of a pair or group. These activities are designed to encourage the rest of the class to look and listen with interest— they really want to know what is going to happen. The result is that students listen with a high level of anticipation and enjoyment. The activities can be done in a traditional classroom setting, where the desks and chairs are in rows. Very occasionally, the desks might be moved to the side of the room for the duration of the activity, but even so, it should be possible to do all these things without too much disruption to the layout of the room.

2.1 Breathing and sound practice

Level Elementary +

Time 5 minutes

Aims To practise individual vowel sounds and intonation.

Preparation

No preparation is required for this activity.

Procedure

1 Ask the class to stand up and make themselves comfortable by shaking their hands, stretching their necks, or by whatever means they would normally use.

2 Tell them to breathe in and, when they breathe out, to make a particular vowel sound.

3 Make sure the sound is being made correctly. Let's imagine you are using the /ɜː/ sound as in word /wɜːd/. Ask them to give you examples of words which contain the sound, e.g. *bird*, *heard*, *early*, *world*, *work* (these all work in RP; the actual words might vary according to the accent of the speaker) and make a list on the board. If they say words which don't contain the sound (*walk*, *old*, *there*, etc.), don't add them to the list, and make a note to revise pronunciation of all these sounds later. See Comment 1 below about different English pronunciations.

4 Tell them you are going to ask them to breathe in again, but this time, when they breathe out, they have to indicate a particular thought or mood with the sound they make. For example, tell them that you want to hear, just in their intonation, the following thought:

I like this very much.

They may be a little confused at first, but give them plenty of chances to do it. In fact, the /ɜː/ sound is not a very good one to indicate this thought or mood (/ɑː/ would be much better), but this is exactly the reason for doing it. The students can do it by raising the pitch of their voice, but you don't need to tell them—the brighter ones will work it out for themselves and the others can copy them.

5 Ask them to breathe in again, and make the /ɜː/ sound again when they breathe out, but this time, tell them to indicate with their intonation the following thought:

I don't like this at all.

This is actually much easier, as the /ɜː/ sound more readily indicates displeasure (and not just for native English speakers—you will be amazed how many speakers of other languages recognize a negative emotion in this sound).

6 The third and last time, when they breathe out, they should try to indicate the following thought:

Are you serious? I don't believe a word of it!

Again, the brighter, more aware students will recognize that this is done with a fall-rise intonation, the almost universal way of indicating doubt and puzzlement.

Comments

1 This activity works regardless of the accent of the teacher, whether native speaker or non-native. The key is to reproduce accurately the vowel sound that you want to use, and to make sure the students have given you correct examples of words which contain the sound.

2.3 Be someone else

Level Elementary +

Time 5–20 minutes

Aims To give students the chance to ask and answer basic personal questions.

Preparation

No preparation is needed for this activity. It does however require a certain level of trust between the teacher and the students, so it is advisable to try this activity with a class you know well.

Procedure

1 Ask a student to come to the front of the class. Tell him/her you are going to ask four questions and you want them answered truthfully. Then ask the following simple questions:

Example *Teacher: What's your name?*
Student: Agnieszka.
Teacher: What nationality are you?
Student: Polish.
Teacher: Where do you live?
Student: Lublin.
Teacher: What do you do?
Student: I'm a student.

2 Now tell 'Agnieszka' that you want her to be someone else. Ask the same four questions and ask her to change the answers to all of them. Don't give her any time to prepare for this.

Example *Teacher: What's your name?*
Student: Monica.
Teacher: What nationality are you?
Student: Irish.
Teacher: Where do you live?
Student: Dublin.
Teacher: What do you do?
Student: I'm a nurse.

3 Now as the rest of the class to ask 'Monica' about her life. Tell them to be careful and not ask questions which are too personal. At this point, you can sit down and be part of the class.

4 There is no rule about how long this questioning should go on—some students think of amazing questions and answers. However, when the questioning starts to slow down, ask 'Monica' to invite another student to the front of the class and continue the procedure. 'Monica' becomes the teacher. She asks the four questions, twice, then she sits down and the questioning begins again.

5 This process can go on for as long or short a time as you think fit. It is worth noting that your role in this activity is minimal, and the focus of the class changes completely.

Follow-up

Written homework. Tell the class to choose one of the characters that they heard about, and write a description of what happened. If the class can use reported speech, then encourage them to do it as a report.

Example *We talked to a nurse from Ireland called Monica. She told us that she enjoyed nursing …*

If they don't know how to write reported speech sentences, encourage them to write it as a dialogue.

Example *Tomas: Do you like nursing?*
Monica: Yes.
Natalia: How long have you been a nurse?
Monica: A year.

Comments

1 This activity is self-regulating. See the note about *Self-regulating improvisations* on page 11.

2 Use the same four questions, regardless of the level of the class and regardless of whether the class is monolingual or multilingual and/ or multi-nationality. And always ask them to give the real answers first. Of course, the answers to questions 2–4 will be almost identical in a monolingual class living in the same town; this does not matter. Giving the real answers gets the students into the rhythm of the activity and gives them a little thinking time.

3 Do not accept answers to the second set of questions if the students want to be a real person, a pop star or sportsperson, for example; this would introduce students' prior knowledge of the person and would interfere with the flow of the activity.

4 When a female student is answering the questions about her new self, there is a tendency for the rest of the class to ask if she is married, or in a relationship. There is nothing wrong with that, but the questioning is then sometimes directed entirely towards the partner and what he does. Try to encourage the questioning to be about the student's new persona, and not other people.

5 Do not worry that you are not giving the students enough preparation time; they will not need it. Even in cultures which are less immediately extrovert, students never fail to come up with a new identity and enter into the spirit of the activity.

2.4 Actions and locations: where are you and what are you doing?

Level Elementary +

Time 10–15 minutes

Aims To practise the present continuous tense and phone language.

Preparation

You need two old mobile phones and two cardboard boxes, or similar containers. Mark the boxes 'A' for 'Actions', and 'L' for 'Locations'. The students need a pen and two pieces of paper.

Procedure

1 Ask the class to write a location on a piece of paper. What you want is a prepositional phrase. Write *on the table* on the board as an example. Encourage them to use different prepositions that they know: *in, under, near, opposite, behind, next to*, etc. Ask the class to fold the papers and put them in a cardboard box, marked 'L' (Locations).

2 Now ask them to write an action on the other piece of paper. The action needs to be in the present continuous tense, but try not to use explanatory grammatical language when you ask them to do this. Write an example on the board: *I'm eating a biscuit.* Indicate that the examples should be in the first person, and there should be a verb and an object. Ask the class to fold the papers and put them in the second cardboard box, marked 'A' (Actions).

3 Invite two students to the front of the class and ask them to stand on either side of the table with the two boxes between them. Give them each a mobile phone. Ask them to begin a normal phone conversation: *Hi, how are you?* etc. Tell them that eventually one of them, Student A, must ask *Where are you?* When Student B hears this question, he/she takes a piece of paper from the 'Locations' box and reads what it says, e.g. *On the beach.* Student A immediately asks *And what are you doing?* Student B takes a piece of paper from the 'Actions' box and reads what it says, e.g. *I'm painting a wall.*

4 You can if you like encourage Student A to ask for more details.

5 Student B now asks Student A the same two questions. Student A takes a piece of paper from each box and reads the contents.

6 The two students then give the mobile phones to two other students, who do exactly the same thing.

This activity can continue, if you wish, until every student in the class has had this mini-conversation. The only argument against allowing everyone to do it is that there may be some written examples that are offensive or illegible, so there may not be enough useable items in the boxes for everyone. (See the note on *Offensive language* on page 12.)

Comments

1 Always make sure they ask *Where are you?* before they ask *What are you doing?* as this tends to lead to a livelier exchange.

2 I have done this activity with the class divided into two queues on either side of the table and it works well. Students simply hand the phones to the people behind them in the queue, then sit down and enjoy the fun. The teacher has to do almost nothing once it gets started and students listen intently. Some of the combinations of action and location are very funny, and the listeners are on the edge of their seats waiting for the next funny one.

2.5 Hobbies and locations

Level Elementary +

Time 15 minutes

Aims To practise likes and dislikes, and questions and answers.

Preparation

As in the previous activity, you need two cardboard boxes or similar containers. Mark them 'H' for 'Hobbies' and 'L' for 'Locations'. The students need a pen and two pieces of paper.

Procedure

1 Ask the students to write a location on one piece of paper. Collect the papers and put them in the box marked 'L' (Locations). See Activity 2.4 Procedure step 1.

2 Now ask them to write a hobby (e.g. *collecting stamps*) on another piece of paper. Before they write anything, brainstorm and write on the board lots of verbs to do with hobbies: *collecting, reading, visiting, watching, making, painting, drawing*, etc. Tell them to write the hobby using the *-ing* form of the verb.

Make sure that they write the locations first. If they write the hobby first and location second, they will probably write a location where the hobby can take place. It is more fun if they do not do this.

3 Collect the papers and put them in a box marked 'H' (Hobbies).

4 Put the two boxes at the front of the class. Ask a student to come to the front of the class and take a piece of paper from the 'Hobbies' box. He/she reads the hobby and says (for example) *My hobby is painting pictures* … He/she then takes a piece of paper from the 'Locations' box and adds (for example) … *in the bathroom*.

5 The rest of the class now ask the student to describe what he/she does and why he/she likes doing it in that particular location. As with the previous activity, it works best if the hobbies and locations are a strange match. The stranger the match, the better. Students really have to improvise reasons why they carry out their hobbies in such an unusual location.

Example *Why do you like painting pictures in the bathroom?*
Because there's a lot of light there.

6 You can if you like limit the number of questions to three. This way, 5–10 students can do this activity in about 15 minutes. The more students who do it, the better!

Comments

Read the note about *Unreal activities* on page 11.

2.6 Find your answer

Level Elementary +

Time 15 minutes

Aims To improve listening and memory skills. To recognize suitable and unsuitable answers to questions.

This activity is similar to a game called Concentration, sometimes known as Pelmanism, which is a system of training to improve the memory, in which you try to match things (usually playing cards) by trial and error.

The point of this activity is for students to find the answer to a question that they have on a piece of paper. They do this by asking their question directly to other students, who have answers on pieces of paper. How you do it depends on the size of your class. If there are 30 students, they have either a question or an answer. More than 30 students are probably too many for this activity. If there are only 10–15 students, they can each have a question and an answer.

Preparation

You need a series of questions and answers on separate pieces of paper. You should provide them, not the students. There is an example 'Find your answer' worksheet on pages 42–43. Photocopy the questions and answers, and cut the paper into strips, each with one question or one answer.

Procedure

1 Put the class into two equal teams, and ask them to stand in lines opposite each other.

2 Let's imagine you have 30 students. You give 15 of them (Team A) a piece of paper with a question on it and the other 15 (Team B) a piece of paper with an answer on it. Tell Team A that they each have to find the person in Team B who is holding the answer to their question.

3 Tell Team A that they will get a chance to ask their question in the order that they are standing. They must not ask their question out of turn, and once they have asked it, they have to wait until the others have asked their questions before they get a second turn.

4 Ask the first person in Team A, Student 1, to ask his/her question directly to someone in Team B. He/she must ask the person by name.

Example *Chen, what do you usually have for breakfast?*

Chen then reads the answer on his piece of paper. It may or may not be the answer that Student 1 wants. If Chen answers *Toast and marmalade*, we can be pretty sure that this is the intended answer. If he answers *Sunshine and a cool breeze*, we can be certain that it is not the intended answer. If it is the wrong answer, Student 1 has to wait until all the other students in Team A have asked their questions before he/she gets another turn.

5 The second student in Team A, Student 2, now asks a question. If Chen has the answer to his/her question, Student 2 can ask him directly. If not, he/she has to ask another student in the line. Again, he/she must address the student by name.

Example   *Susana, where did you meet that interesting man?*

Susana gives her answer. If it is the correct answer, Student 2 and Susana sit down. If it is not, Student 2 has to wait for another turn.

6   The point is that everyone in Team B has an answer which is correct for someone in Team A. When the students in Team A hear any answer, someone should recognize it as the answer to their question. But they must all wait their turn to ask their questions. Team A ask their questions in the order that they are standing.

7   The game continues until every student in Team A has matched their answer with someone in Team B.

Follow-up

Tell the people with matching questions and answers to sit together, and ask them to devise a longer sketch or conversation based on this opening question and answer.

Comments

1   The answers are: 1 e; 2 a; 3 j; 4 c; 5 h; 6 d; 7 f; 8 l; 9 b; 10 g; 11 o; 12 i; 13 n; 14 m; 15 k.

2   Some students do not seem to be able to hear the connection between their question and the right answer, or they notice who has the answer, but then cannot remember who it was when it is their turn to ask. This is apparently a common feature of Pelmanism activities, and it reinforces the value of games such as this at making students concentrate.

3   The term 'Pelmanism' has its origin at the Pelman Institute in London, where the card version of this game originated in the nineteenth century, as part of a memory education programme. There are several online free downloads if you want to try the card game yourself. You can find a good example at www.vazcarreiro.net/Pelmanism24.html.

4   You can if you prefer do this as a mingling activity. Students walk round the class until they find the answer to their question. But it is much more fun if they can hear all the mis-matched questions and answers. And as a mingler, it does not have the value of the Pelmanism activity.

Worksheet 2.6

1 What do you usually have for breakfast?	a At my sister's wedding.
2 Where did you meet that interesting man?	b Sitting in front of the TV with my feet up.
3 Where do you keep important papers?	c In the back of a taxi, I think.
4 Where did you lose your umbrella?	d My cousin Alex.
5 What weather do you like best?	e Toast and marmalade.
6 Who's your favourite family member?	f Bananas, coconuts, and palm oil.
7 What's the main export of Nicaragua?	g The marathon race.

8 What do you like on your pizza?	h Sunshine and a cool breeze.	
9 What do you like doing when you finish work?	i Leonardo DiCaprio.	
10 What is your country's most successful sport at the Olympics?	j In a cupboard next to my bed.	
11 Where do you like to relax?	k Smoking cigarettes and shouting.	
12 Who is your favourite film star?	l Cheese, tomatoes, onions, and mushrooms.	
13 What's the capital of Turkey?	m More than a billion.	
14 How many people live in China?	n I think it's Ankara.	
15 What kind of behaviour do you most hate?	o In a sauna or steam room.	

2.7 Blocking activities

Level Elementary +

Time 5–15 minutes

Aims To practise dealing politely with unwanted requests and invitations.

There are three classic blocking activities used by actors when they do improvisation training.

- *I'm afraid you can't.*
- *I'm afraid I can't.*
- *Yes, but …*

In the following procedures, I have tried to make these very interesting and thought-provoking drama training activities accessible for English students. The three activities are connected, but it is not intended that all three should be done at the same time.

Preparation

Students need a pen and paper. No other preparation is required.

Procedure

A: I'm afraid you can't.

1 Tell the students to write down three desires, beginning *I want to …* or *I'd like to …*

Tell them to leave a space to write something between the three examples.

Example *I'd like to visit the cathedral.*

_____

I want to buy a new dictionary.

_____

I want to eat something.

_____

2 Now tell them to walk round the class expressing their desires, one by one, to different students. When someone expresses a desire to you, you have to block it and give a reason. The result is a series of mini-dialogues.

Example A: *I'd like to visit the cathedral.*
B: *I'm afraid you can't.*
A: *Why not?*
B: *It's closed today.*

Student B then expresses his/her desire, and is similarly politely blocked. Both students then write down the reason why they can't do what they want to do in the space under the desire on their piece of paper.

3 Students only express one desire to any other student. When both students have been blocked, they mingle again and express their second desire to another student. They are politely blocked, they ask the reason and write it down.

4 When each student has expressed all three of their desires, they then go back to the first desire. This next part is important! When they have their fourth mini-conversation, they are expressing the first desire again. This time, they are allowed to challenge the block if it is the same as the block they received the first time round. They can prove it by showing what they wrote down the first time they were blocked in this way. Student B must give a different reason. So, now there will be mini-conversations.

Example *A: I'd like to visit the cathedral.*
B: I'm afraid you can't.
A: Why not?
B: It's closed today.
A: Sorry, I've already heard that!
B: OK. I'm afraid you can't because they are repairing the roof.

It is not necessary to write down the second reason. When students have expressed all three desires twice, the activity can end.

B: I'm afraid I can't.

1 In this case, students write down three invitations on a piece of paper.

Example *Would you like to come to the cinema tonight?*

_____

Would you like to have a coffee after class?

_____

Would you like to watch a DVD with me?

_____

If you are doing this activity with teenagers, you may wish to monitor the note-writing to ensure that they are not writing anything offensive.

2 Now tell them to walk round the class expressing their invitations, one by one, to different students. When someone invites you to do something, you have to block it and give a reason. Once again, the result is a series of mini-dialogues.

Example *A: Would you like to come to the cinema tonight?*
B: I'm afraid I can't.
A: Why not?
B: I have a lot of homework.

Student B then expresses his/her invitation, and is similarly politely blocked. Both students then write down the reason why they can't do what they want in the space under the invitation on their piece of paper.

3 The activity continues in the same way as *I'm afraid I can't.*

C: Yes, but …

1 This is different from the previous two, but also requires students to think on their feet. Basically, students ask each other a series of inverted questions, in other words, questions that can be answered *Yes* or *No*. However, the aim is not to answer the questions truthfully, but to answer *Yes, but …*

2 Before the students mingle and do this themselves, help them to understand how it works by asking some questions, and requesting a *Yes, but …* reply. Here are some useful examples, with answers that you might hear.

Examples *Teacher: Do you speak English?*
Student: Yes, but not very well.

Teacher: Are you Spanish?
Student: Yes, but my mother is Portuguese.

Teacher: Are you going out this evening?
Student: Yes, but I have to do some homework first.

Teacher: Do you like Italian food?
Student: Yes, but I don't know how to cook it.

3 Let the students mingle and ask each other questions.

2.8 Famous person interview

Level Intermediate +

Time 10–15 minutes

Aims To practise questions and answers. To provide a guessing game for other students in the class.

Preparation

No preparation is required for this activity. Points are involved, so you need to keep score on the board.

Procedure

1 Put the class in pairs. Ask each pair quietly to choose a famous person, someone that everyone in the class will have heard of. In a monolingual class who all live in the same town, this can be someone local, but encourage the class to think of people from other countries. Tell them that they should also invent a reason why the famous person is in your town.

2 Tell each pair to pretend that one of them is the famous person, and the other is a journalist. They are going to do a celebrity interview for the rest of the class but they won't use the name of the person during the interview. The aim of the activity is for the rest of the class to guess who the famous person is.

3 Each pair quietly practises some questions and answers that they can use. One of the things they can talk about is why the famous person is visiting your town. Walk round the class and listen to the

preparations, and remind them that they must not use the name of the person during the interview. For example, the interviewer doesn't start by saying *I'm talking to Brad Pitt about his latest film.*

4 When all the pairs are ready, ask for volunteers or select a pair to begin. Tell the rest of the class to listen. When someone thinks they know who the celebrity is, they put up their hand and say: *I know!* This is important—you should discourage students from mumbling names as they listen. If anyone says a name without first putting up their hand and saying *I know!*, they lose a point.

5 If someone says *I know!*, the interview pauses, and the student says who they think the celebrity is. If he/she is right, his/her team gets a point. If he/she is wrong, the team loses a point, and the interview continues until someone else puts up their hand.

6 Write the name of the teams on the board. As points are won or lost, add or subtract points from their scores.

Follow-up

This is another good activity for practising reported speech, either in a post-activity discussion or for written homework. Students can write details of one or more of the interviews.

Example   *Laszlo interviewed Cameron Diaz. He asked her why she was here in our town and she replied that …*

Comments

In my experience, some students go to great lengths to make it difficult for others to guess who the celebrity is. They often choose dead celebrities, or people who are the opposite sex, or cartoon characters. I think this is good, and any sense of frustration is short-lived and adds to the atmosphere. And again, the rest of the class listen intently to what is being said.

2.9 Secrets and lies

Level   Intermediate +

Time   15 minutes

Aims   To practise questions and answers and the art of evasion.

Preparation

No preparation is needed for this activity.

Procedure

1 Ask everyone in the class to write down a series of questions that they might ask someone that they want to get to know better. Encourage them to ask unusual questions, but remind them not to be offensive or too personal. Elicit a few imaginative examples and write them on the board to get them started.

Examples   *Who is your hero?*
What skill would you like to have that you don't have now?

What do you think is important in a relationship?
Have you ever done something you regretted?

2   When they have written 5–10 questions, put the students in pairs. Ask them to choose who is going to be the first questioner, Student A.

3   Tell Student A to ask his/her questions as quickly as he/she can. Student B answers the questions, alternating between true answers and lies. Student B must not hesitate or laugh, and must keep strictly to the alternation, one true answer, one false answer.

4   If and when Student B hesitates or laughs, or clearly fails to alternate between truth and lies, the partners reverse roles.

5   As an extra idea, each student can have the option of saying *That's a secret!* to avoid answering one of the questions.

Comments

Like many activities in this book, this works best if pairs 'perform' for the rest of the class. Let all the pairs practise together, but then ask for volunteers to do the asking and answering in front of the rest of the class.

2.10 Duelling stories

Level   Intermediate +

Time   15 minutes

Aims   To describe a film or television programme.

Preparation

Students make notes about a film, play or television programme that they have recently seen. It helps if they write the story (or details of the television programme if it was a documentary, for example) for homework, so they have the details on paper in front of them while they do the activity. If it is not done for homework, then students will need some time to write down the main points in class.

Procedure

1   Divide the class into pairs. Tell them that they are going to tell their partner about the film or television programme that they have made notes about. First of all, they take it in turns to read from their notes. The listener can ask questions or make observations about what he/she hears.

2   When they have both had time to tell the story and listen to their partner's story, the duelling starts. Tell them you are going to give them a minute to re-tell their story. They will have to do it without notes, staring their partner in the eye—and they are both going to tell their story at the same time. If necessary, they can shout to drown out the other person's story. If one of them laughs, gives up, or runs out of story before the minute is complete, the other is the winner.

3 Count down to the start of the minute and shout *Go!*

Follow-up

Give the students the chance to say how they feel about the second part of this activity. Some of them—alpha types—will love the challenge, others will feel frustrated and annoyed by it. Discuss the good and bad points about being able to dominate a conversation in this way. Was the first way of telling the story (reading from notes without interruption) more useful?

2.11 Who's that?

Level Intermediate +

Time 15 minutes

Aims To practise questions and answers. To practise the present perfect for achievement, or with *just*.

Preparation

No preparation is needed for this activity.

Procedure

1 Brainstorm a list of celebrity occupations. Write them on the board. Encourage the class to think of examples beyond the obvious celebrity occupations of *singer, actor,* and *footballer*: *writer, politician, research scientist, journalist, athlete, poet,* etc.

2 Put the class into groups of 4–6. Tell them that they are at a party where everyone is famous.

3 Students now ask the question *Who's that?* to people in their own group about people in other groups. Explain that when someone asks you this question, you should invent a celebrity occupation and other information for the person they are talking about. *She's a famous pop star from Spain. He's an Olympic runner from the USA,* etc. Encourage students to give extra information about them: *She's recorded an album with Justin Timberlake. He's just made his first film.*

4 Each group should talk about at least one person from each of the other groups. Tell them not to talk about real famous people. Walk round the groups to check that they are doing the activity correctly.

5 Now ask the students to split up and mingle with other groups. They should approach someone they have been talking about in their own group and engage him/her in conversation. They should ask a question they have always wanted to ask.

6 The people who are being questioned of course have no idea what kind of celebrity they are supposed to be until they are approached. When someone engages in conversation with them, however, they must 'accept and add'. (See Comment 1.) In other words, if someone says that you are a famous scientist, you must be a famous scientist. It will get a laugh if you say *Actually, I'm a road-sweeper,* but it doesn't help the activity.

Example *Student 1: Hello, I've always wanted to meet you!*
Student 2: Really? Why?
Student 1: Because I love your movies. Are you making one now?
Student 2: Yes, we're making a film about pirates.

It is possible of course that this conversation may be interrupted by someone else who wants to talk to the same celebrity. The second person will probably have a completely different persona in mind, and might start asking this film actor/director about his political career! This is not a problem—the interviewee now has to respond to those questions as well.

Follow-up

When the students are all back in their seats, ask people to say who they were in this simulation. When some of them have multiple personas, it can be very amusing to hear them.

Example *I'm captain of the national football team and I'm also a space explorer.*

Comments

1 See the note about *Accept and add* on page 11.

2 Of all the activities in this section, this is the one which is most likely to be a little chaotic. Think carefully before you do it—is your classroom suited to this amount of movement? Will teachers in neighbouring classes be upset by the noise?

2.12 Fishbowl

Level Intermediate +

Time 10–30 minutes

Aims To create a series of improvised exchanges.

Preparation

You need a cardboard box or similar container. Students need a pen and a large piece of paper, which they will cut into three pieces.

Procedure

1 Tell students to get three small pieces of paper. Tell them that they are going to write three separate conversation items on the pieces of paper. Ask them to write clearly as other people may have to read what they write.

2 Ask them to write a STATEMENT on the first one. Tell them that you want conversation items, e.g. *I saw a good television programme yesterday*, not something you might hear in a speech, e.g. *The main agricultural produce of this country is corn.*

3 Ask them to write a QUESTION on the second piece of paper. They may ask if the statement and question should be related, and you can tell them that it doesn't matter whether it is or not.

4 Ask them to write an EXCLAMATION on the third piece of paper. If they don't understand what you mean, give an example: *Oh no!* Tell them not to use the example you give, they must think of another one.

5 Ask them to fold up the three pieces of paper and put them all in the same box. Put the box on a chair or table at the front of the class, and put a chair on either side of it.

6 Ask for two volunteers to sit in the chairs. Tell them they are going to have a conversation. First of all, the rest of the class have to provide a context for the conversation. Ask the rest of the class the following three questions to provide information about the two volunteers:

Who are these people?
Where are they?
What are they talking about?

The class should come up with a situation that is clear to everyone.

Example *They are neighbours.*
They are standing in the street.
They are talking about another neighbour.

7 Ask the two students to begin a conversation in these roles. Tell the rest of the class that, if the conversation begins to slow down, they can shout *Fish!* If this happens, one of the students takes a piece of paper from the box and reads what it says. The two students must find a way of incorporating this new line into their conversation. Thereafter, the two students take it in turns to take a piece of paper from the box.

8 A good rule is that they should be allowed three lines from the box each. If their conversation becomes absolutely hilarious, allow them to continue. Eventually, thank the pair and ask them to go back to their seats. Ask for two more volunteers. Ask the rest of the class to provide new characters, location, and conversation topic for them.

9 Repeat the activity for as long as you want, or until the box is empty.

Comments

1 There is potential for activities like this to backfire. For example, in this case, the topic of conversation which is suggested by the rest of the class may be limited, obscure, too personal, or potentially offensive. If this is the case, feel free to ask for other suggestions. But, as far as possible, allow the students to provide input without teacher interference.

2 Read the notes about *Student suspicion* on page 9 and *Students who talk too much* on page 11.

3 Try to discourage the class from shouting *Fish!* too often.

2.13 Superhero, household object, and location

Level Intermediate +

Time 15 minutes

Aims To create an improvised narrative story.

Preparation

You need either four or five volunteers. No other preparation is needed for this activity.

Procedure

1 Choose four or five volunteers, who will be a team of three or four, plus a director. Tell them that they are going to tell a story.

2 The three or four members of the team sit in a line in front of the class. The director sits facing them. If circumstances permit, the director can sit on the floor.

3 You then ask the rest of the class to give you the three items which must appear in the story: a superhero, a household object, and a location, e.g. Superman, a vacuum cleaner, and Central Park, New York.

4 Tell the director to point at one member of the team. That person must start a story which will eventually involve Superman, a vacuum cleaner, and Central Park. If and when he/she slows down or hesitates, the director points the finger at another team member, who continues the story. In fact, the director can point at another member of the team at any point, and the new member must take up the story from that point. In this way, no one is exposed or embarrassed, and the rest of the class watch with interest as the story unfolds.

Follow-up

With a somewhat chaotic narrative like this one, I would not recommend writing the story for homework. A much better idea is for the class to write it down immediately. They then get into groups and compare what they have written. The team who told the story can take a rest after their exertions, and can be monitors of the writing activity.

2.14 Tourist guide

Level Intermediate +

Time 15–20 minutes

Aims To practise question forms and describing places. To practise the passive in a free practice activity.

Preparation

You need a number of tourist picture postcards. The postcards should show tourist sites from around the world, and it is better if they are lesser-known ones. It is also useful if there is no indication of the location on the picture side of the card. In other words, the picture that the students can see should have no writing on it, or at least no city name.

The number of postcards you need depends on the size of the class. You are going to put the class into groups, preferably of 4–6, and you need as many postcards as there are groups. Fix the postcards to the wall of the classroom, all around the room (not too close to each other).

It also helps if the class know how to use the passive voice. You may want to remind them of the kind of passive sentences that are used to describe places of tourist interest.

Examples *The city is surrounded by forests.*
It is situated on a river/near the sea.
It was designed by Le Corbusier.
It's inhabited by a group of artists.
It was built in 1900.
It was invaded by the Romans.
It was destroyed by fire.
An important treaty was signed there.

Procedure

1 Indicate the picture postcards on the wall around the room and tell the students that they are all going to be tourists, and they are all going to be tour guides, too. Emphasize that they do not have to know anything about the places in the pictures. In fact, it is better if they know nothing at all about them.

2 Put the students into as many groups as there are cards on the wall, or almost as many. Preferably the number of people in the group should be more or less the same as the number of cards. In other words, if there are 30 students in the class, you could put them into five groups of six, and have six or seven postcards on the wall.

3 Tell each group to stand in front of a postcard. One person in the group is the first tour guide. You can, if you like, nominate the first one, but it is better if you tell someone in the group to ask a direct question about the place in the postcard to another member of the group: *Can you tell me something about this church?* The person who is asked becomes the tour guide and talks about the building, monument, or landscape in the picture.

4 Tell the tourists to continue asking questions. When the questions begin to die down, ask all the groups to move to the next postcard.

5 When they are all in position at the next postcard, the tour guide from the first postcard asks a direct question to another member of the group, who becomes the second tour guide. Tell the group to ask more questions. When the questions begin to die down, tell all the groups to move to the next postcard.

6 Continue this procedure until the groups have visited all the cards, or until everyone has had the chance to be a tour guide.

Follow-up

When the students have returned to their seats, point at the postcards one by one, and ask what the students learnt about them. Compare and contrast the different invented stories about each location. If the students really want to know, you can tell them where the tourist attractions really are. However, discourage any self-congratulation on the part of any tour guide who was right!

Comments

1 See the note on *Shy and quiet students* on page 10.

2 Tell the students they must not question any of the information that they hear, even if they know it is wrong. For example, if the postcard shows a picture of Paris, and the guide says that it is Rome, then for the purposes of the activity, it *is* Rome. The language being practised, and the improvisation of the answers, is much more important than 'the truth'.

3 Some groups will be more talkative than others, but you need to go at the speed of the quieter groups. When most of the groups have run out of questions, it's time to move on, even if one or two of the groups are still asking questions.

2.15 Experts

Level Intermediate +

Time 10–30 minutes

Aims To practise structuring sentences in the context of a game.

Preparation

No preparation is needed for this activity.

Procedure

1 Put three chairs in front of the class and ask for three volunteers to sit in them.

2 Tell the three people in the chairs that they are experts, but we don't know yet what they are experts about.

3 Ask the class to choose a topic that the three students are experts about. The first time, accept simple and easily understood topics like *Food*, *Films*, or *Sport*. Let's say you choose *Food*. Tell the three volunteers that they are now experts about food and they are going to answer questions from the class about this topic. However, it is not quite as straightforward as that. When they answer the questions, they have to do it one word at a time, in sequence.

Example *Student A: I …*
Student B: think …
Student C: that …
Student A: it's …

4 Invite the rest of the class to ask the experts a question about the chosen topic.

Examples *What is the most difficult dish to cook?*
What is the healthiest food to eat?

The three experts then try to answer the question. Let them make their answer as long or as short as they like.

5 Let the class ask a maximum of three questions to the experts, then choose three new experts and a new topic for them. Continue the game for as long as you can allow.

Comments

Accept contractions—*I'm, it's, don't,* etc.—as one word.

2.16 Alphabet story

Level Intermediate +

Time 10–15 minutes

Aims To develop a spoken narrative that can then be the basis of a written narrative and/or a short drama. To practise past tense forms.

Preparation

No preparation is needed for this activity, but it works best if the students are sitting in a circle.

Procedure

1 Tell the class that they are going to develop a narrative story, line by line.

2 Ask students to come up with a title for the story. You may if you wish give them a few moments to discuss this in pairs or groups. A narrative story of course works better if it is about an event or incident in the past, so the title could refer to a person, an incident or event, a place and/or a time in the past. If the class are unable to think of a title, write the following examples on the board and ask them to choose or amend one.

Examples *A strange incident on a train*
An unusual holiday
Someone I met last summer
Robbery at the hotel
The mystery of the black suitcase

3 Now tell the class that the story is going to be an alphabet story and that they are all going to contribute to it. In an alphabet story, each line must start with the letter of the alphabet which follows the starting letter of the previous line. If the story starts like this:

A strange thing happened on a train last week …

then the next line must start with the letter 'B':

Bernard Smith got on the train at his usual station.

4 Ask for a volunteer to start the story, or choose someone. Ask them which letter of the alphabet they would like to start with (they do not have to start with A). Then proceed with the story.

Follow-up

I do not usually suggest acting out as a follow-up to the activities in this chapter, because there are plenty of acting out opportunities in other places in the book. However, this is an exception because when the class finishes the story, there is a wonderful opportunity to act out the story that they have told. You can do this instantly. Put the class into groups of however many characters emerged from the story. Ask them either to act out the narrative they have heard, or to act out what happened next.

Comments

1 A narrative story can consist of a lot of dialogue. Do not insist on the class using reported speech in their lines if they find it easier to move the story along with a line of dialogue.

2 If you are able to put the class in a circle, and students are all more or less the same level of ability, it is quite interesting to tell the story one by one round the circle. On the other hand, if you wish to protect the weaker students in your class, you can let the story develop as a free-for-all.

3 You can help the class by giving them some advice about how to think of a word beginning with a particular letter. In a narrative past tense story, some letters are easy: I (I), H (he), S (she), T (then), L (later), Y (yes), N (no), A (and), B (but). For other letters, tell them they can if they wish introduce a new character whose name begins with the letter they have to use. Allow words beginning *ex-* when they reach the letter X.

3
Fun and games

The activities in this chapter all involve some kind of movement. They are perfect to break up a lesson where students would otherwise sit at their desks for an hour or longer. They do not take long to do and will unquestionably improve the overall atmosphere of the class.

Although everyone seems to agree that primary school pupils need to move around during their lessons, fewer people are convinced by arguments in favour of kinaesthetic activities for secondary students, college students, and adults. The arguments are mainly that they are disruptive and 'most older students don't like moving around'. However, students of all ages tend to under-perform if they stay motionless for an hour or more.

Adult students do occasionally need to move around, to change focus and to become energized by a fun and/or kinaesthetic activity, just as much as primary school pupils. There are of course teenagers and adults who would prefer to sit and read and not move about, but they are in the minority.

You may hear some grumbling if you ask adult students to get up and move around, but—unless you are very unlucky—they will return to their seats energized and smiling. They are then in the right mood to do some more 'serious' learning—unlike primary pupils, who just want to continue playing!

As stated on pages 8–9, the terms 'ice-breakers' and 'warmers' have been avoided, because these expressions suggest that you should only use these activities at the beginning of a course or the beginning of a class. Although ice-breaker activities are indeed important with a new class, it is not necessarily the case that most classes need an activity to 'warm them up' when they arrive. Quite the reverse, in fact. Many teenagers arrive in class full of energy and need an activity that will calm them down, and adult learners tend to want to do something serious when they arrive.

However, there will come a moment in every lesson when the students, whatever age they are, will start to tire. This is no reflection on your teaching. Learning a foreign language—speaking, reading, writing, and thinking in another language for an extended period— can be stimulating but also very tiring. When the class starts to flag, it may be the right time for one of the following activities.

In some of the activities, moving the furniture around in the classroom is recommended. If this is impossible, either because the furniture is fixed or because of school rules, you may not be able to do them. If there is an alternative way of doing it, which does not involve moving the furniture, this is noted.

3.1 Typewriter game

Level Elementary +

Time 10 minutes

Aims To revise spelling in a kinaesthetic way.

carriage
return
lever

This is a game where students clap out the spelling of given words.

Preparation

First of all, you need to explain how an old-fashioned typewriter works. Explain that before electronic keyboards, people used to type on a machine which made a loud noise when each letter was pressed. In addition, when typists reached the end of a line on the page, they had to operate something called the 'carriage return lever', to get back to the start of the next line. This is important to know, because a key element in the activity is the sound of the carriage return lever. Ideally, you need at least 26 students for this activity, and each one has a different letter of the alphabet. You can of course do it with fewer participants, and students can have more than one letter. In fact, it is better if this happens, because if all the students have only one letter, then the person with 'x' or 'z' may not get many chances to participate. If there are more than 26 students in the class, some students will have to share a letter.

It works best if the students stand or sit in a circle or in such a way that they can see each other. Finally, it helps if you ask students to write their letter or letters on a piece of paper which they can attach to their shirt, so people can check the spelling as they watch.

Procedure

1 Assign each student a letter or letters of the alphabet. Explain that you are going to say a word, and they have to spell it out by clapping their hands. For example, if you say the word CLASSROOM, the students who are C, L, A, S, R, O, and M have to clap their hands. Obviously, the students who are S and O have to clap their hands twice in succession. The rest of the class listen, working out the spelling in their heads. After the student who is M has clapped, everyone claps twice (the sound of the carriage return lever).

2 There may be 'spelling mistakes'. Someone may forget to clap, or wait for a letter that is not there, or clap at the same time as someone else. Sometimes a student double-claps alone thinking the word has ended before it actually has. Tell the class not to worry about this and it is not a problem if they have to start again. It can be quite useful when this happens.

3 If you like, you can ask students to come to the front of the class and shout out the words. They should still have letters of course, so they have to clap when it is their turn.

Variation

An alternative to the clapping game is as follows: the same situation applies, the students have one or two letters each. This time, when the word is shouted out, they have to run to the front of the class or to the middle of the circle and spell the word out with their bodies. If there's a double letter, like the 's' and 'o' in 'classroom', the person who 'is' that letter must jump from side to side to indicate that there are two letters. If the letter occurs twice separately in a word, the person whose letter it is must run in a circle connecting the two spaces where the letter goes. Again, it helps if the students have the letters pinned to their clothing, so that the rest of the class can check the spelling.

Follow-up

During the activity itself, the words are not seen, only shouted out. At the end of the activity, the teacher should ask people to remember all the words that were used, and write them on the board. After the confusion and mayhem of this very physical activity, this quiet follow-up makes sure students get the spelling right.

Comments

It is possible to do these activities without moving the chairs into a circle. Students can clap their hands without leaving their seats for the first activity. For the variation, they can run (or move quickly) to the front of the class to spell out the word.

3.2 Holding hands

Level Elementary +

Time 15 minutes

Aim To practise spelling. To energize a class which has been sitting still for a long time.

This activity requires the teacher to hold hands with students. If you are not happy with this idea, you can ask a student to take the teacher's role below.

Preparation

Place chairs in two lines facing each other, at most eight chairs in a line. If there are more than 16 students in the class, you need three or four lines of chairs. 32 is really the maximum number that can do this activity. If you have 24 students, you can have four lines of six, but fewer than six will not work as well. You can work out the mathematics after you read the instructions.

You need to write eight long words on a flip chart or on the board. If the words are on the board, they should be in the middle. Number the words 1—8. The words should be known to the students, but preferably long and with unusual spellings. On the board, you should also write Team A and Team B (and Team C and D if there are four teams). If the words are in the middle of the board, write the team names on the left and right. If you like, ask the teams to think of a name for themselves and write the team name on the board.

There should be chalk or a white board marker for all the teams. At the beginning of the activity, the chalk or marker should be in the hand of the last person in the team, the person furthest away from the teacher.

Here is a typical list of words that can be used in the activity.

Example 1 ELECTRICITY
2 INCOMPREHENSIBLE
3 AUTOMATICALLY
4 INDECISIVE
5 SUPERMARKET
6 METEOROLOGY
7 UNIVERSAL
8 IMMIGRATION

Now ask the students to sit in the rows of chairs facing each other.

Procedure

1 Ask the students to hold hands with the people next to them in their team (not with the people they are facing!). Tell them to look at the list of words on the board or flip chart.

2 Explain that you are going to hold hands with the first person in each team. You are going to squeeze their hands a number of times—between one and eight times. The first person must squeeze the second person's hands the same number of times, and so on until the squeezes reach the last person in the line, the one furthest away from the teacher.

3 The last person in each row then runs to the board and writes the word which corresponds to the number of squeezes. With the words in the example list above, if the last person in the team feels seven squeezes, he/she writes UNIVERSAL on the board. The student who writes the word first gets a point for his/her team, as long as the word is correctly spelt. However, the students in each team may write different words, because they have misinterpreted the number of squeezes. You then have to tell them which word you 'squeezed'.

4 Everyone in the team now moves down a chair, and the person who wrote on the board now sits at the top of the team, after giving the board pen or chalk to the student who is now at the end of the line.

5 The teacher repeats the action. Squeeze the hands of the first people in the teams. Squeeze a different number of times, so they have to pass on a different word. When the last person in the team feels the squeeze, he/she runs to the board and writes the word.

6 Continue until everyone in the team has had at least one chance to write on the board.

Follow-up

If you see from the writing on the board that some of the words have been misspelt, remind students of the correct spelling. Then ask people to work in their teams and write a short story using all the words.

Comments

If there are three or four rows of chairs, then obviously someone else will have to hold hands with teams three and four. You need to appoint a student-helper to do this. Choose a student, and then oversee the initial set-up of the other team or teams before you start. Then choose a word and whisper it to your helper.

3.3 Adjective mime

Level Elementary +

Time 10–15 minutes

Aims To revise adjectives. To energize the class through a mime activity.

Preparation

Put two chairs in front of the board, but facing away from it. Put the class into two teams. If there are more than 20 students in the class, you may need to make three teams.

Procedure

1 After you have divided the class into teams, ask one person from each team to sit in the chair facing away from the board.

2 Now ask someone from Team A to write an adjective on the board behind Team B's seat, and someone from Team B to write an adjective on the board behind Team A's seat. Do not pay attention to spelling at this stage—you can do something about that later.

3 The teams now have to mime the adjective until the person in the chair gets it right. The first team to get it right gets a point. Let the second team continue until their person has also guessed the adjective.

4 Someone else from each team now sits in the chair, and each team writes a new adjective on the board. Continue the process until there are ten adjectives in each list.

Variation

If you prefer, you can call it 'Adverb mime', and ask people to write adverbs on the board. The person in the chair can then ask people to perform actions suggested by the adverb to help him/her guess what it is. You can also do it with nouns. I have tried all three, and in my opinion, adjectives offer the best opportunities for interesting mimes.

Follow-up

You now have around 20 adjectives or adverbs on the board. Now check that they are all spelt correctly. Ask the whole class to read the adjectives and check the spelling. This ensures that no one remembers who wrote any particular adjective, so no one is 'guilty' of bad spelling.

3.4 What am I wearing?

Level Elementary +

Time 15 minutes

Aims To test memory. To revise the present and past continuous tenses. To revise clothing vocabulary.

Preparation

No preparation is needed for this activity.

Procedure

1 Ask two students, Student A and Student B, to stand back-to-back. Tell them to describe the other person from memory. Ask them specifically to say what the other person is wearing. Encourage other students in the class to ask for details.

Example *Student A: She's wearing a T-shirt.*
Rest of class: What colour is it?

2 Encourage the rest of the class to ask them for details of things they have not mentioned, particularly watches, rings, and other jewellery.

3 At this point, you can invite one or two students to act as helpers for Student A and Student B. The helpers should not speak, but they can mime things that the two have forgotten.

4 If you like, you can begin the activity with the helpers in position.

5 Two students plus helpers can do this activity in a few minutes. You can do the activity twice in ten minutes. Decide if you want more students to do this, or end the activity here.

Variation

Invite two students to the front of the class and ask them to make a mental note of details of the other person's appearance. Then ask them to turn away from each other and, with the help of another student if necessary, make three small changes to their appearance.

Examples *take off a tie*
fasten or unfasten a button on shirt or blouse
take off ring, ear rings, necklace, or watch
change ring or watch from one finger/hand to the other
roll up sleeves

The students then face each other again and try to describe what the three changes in the other student are. This is good practice for the present continuous and past continuous tenses.

Example *You're wearing your watch on your right wrist now. Before, you were wearing it on your left wrist.*

Follow-up

After one pair of students have done the activity in front of the class, divide the class into pairs and ask them all to do it.

3.5 Yes/No game

Level Elementary +

Time 15 minutes

Aims To practise questions and answers.

In this activity, students have to answer questions without saying *yes* or *no*.

Preparation

You need a volunteer to indicate that someone has said *yes* or *no*, or that they have reached a minute. To do this, the volunteer needs something that makes a noise. A whistle will work but something like a bicycle bugle horn is ideal. The funnier the noise, the better!

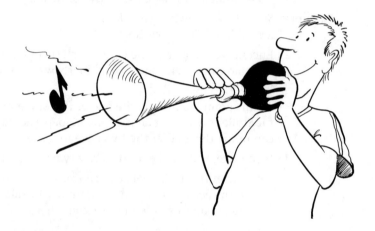

Procedure

1 Ask for two volunteers—one to keep time and one to make a noise (with the bugle horn for example) when someone says *yes* or *no*, and/or when the minute is completed.

2 Explain to the students that you are going to ask one of them questions for one minute and they have to answer the questions without saying *yes* or *no*.

3 Ask for a volunteer to come and answer your questions. Make it easy to start with by asking *Wh-* questions that do not usually elicit a *yes/no* response.

Examples *What's your name?*
How old are you?
What's your favourite colour?
Who is your favourite movie star?
Where do you live?
What time did you get up?
What did you have for breakfast?

Some of the above questions are unsuitable for certain groups, of course. Adult students are sometimes not happy to reveal their age, and some teenagers are embarrassed about where they live. You will know which questions are appropriate for your own students.

4 When the student is feeling relaxed and confident, you can ask an inverted question that could elicit a *yes/no* response.

Examples *Are you hungry?*
Do you like spaghetti?
Were you at school yesterday?
Did you watch television last night?

5 If someone says *yes/no*, give them another chance to answer the question. Suggest ways that they can avoid using *yes* or *no*.

Examples *Are you hungry?*
I AM hungry, that's right.
Do you like spaghetti?
I DON'T like spaghetti, in fact.

6 Play the game with two or three students, then ask for a volunteer or nominate someone to take the role of questioner from you. Generally speaking, keep giving volunteers another chance, so they all continue to answer questions for a minute.

Follow-up

You may find all kinds of things that need revising after an activity like this. Students usually make mistakes with question forms and tenses when they do it.

3.6 Language rules race

Level Intermediate +

Time 15 minutes

Aims To revise grammar in a noisy and kinaesthetic way.

The idea of this activity is that you are going to read out language 'rules' or statements. Some of them will be true, and some false. Students have to decide if they are true or false very quickly.

Preparation

Ideally, you need to clear a space in the middle of the room and put a chair at each end. One of the chairs should have a sign saying TRUE, and the other should have a sign saying FALSE.

You then divide the class into two teams, and give each person in the team a number. So, if there are 20 students in the class, there will be two teams of ten and each student will have a number between one and ten.

If it's impossible for time or logistic reasons to move the furniture, then the two teams can stand against the walls of the room. Be careful! Make sure that they don't trip each other up when they run to the chairs.

You need to make a list of true and false language rules or more general statements about language. A suggested list is given below. The great advantage of this game is that you can tailor it to meet the needs of your students, so that the examples reflect what the class have been doing recently.

Procedure

1 Explain to the two teams that you are going to read out a language 'rule' or statement, which may be true or false. You will then say a number. The students in the two teams with that number then run to the TRUE chair if they think the rule/statement is true, and to the FALSE chair if they think it is false.

2 Before you start the game, give them a simple example: *The past tense of the verb 'give' is 'gived'.* Explain to the students that if they think it's false, they run to the FALSE chair. The first one to sit in the chair gets a point for the team, but only if they can say why the statement is false. If the statement is true, then they get a point by being the first to reach the TRUE chair.

3 Ask the teams to get ready and then read out the first language rule or statement. Here are some that you can use, but it is best if you write your own, bearing in mind what your class have been working on recently.

Examples *The comparative form of all adjectives ends in '-er'.* FALSE
All plural nouns end in 's'. FALSE
There is more than one pronunciation for the letters O-U-G-H. TRUE
You always have to use 'an' before a noun which starts with a vowel. FALSE
The difference between 'say' and 'tell' is that 'tell' needs an object. TRUE
'Next to' and 'near' mean the same thing. FALSE
You use 'do' when you make questions with 'can' and 'must'. FALSE
You can use 'too' before a noun. FALSE
You 'do homework' but you 'make a cake'. TRUE
You can use the present simple tense to talk about routines. TRUE
The past tense and past participle of the verb 'drive' are the same. FALSE
The past tense of 'teach' rhymes with the past tense of 'think'. TRUE

The students may run to different chairs, which is actually quite helpful as it means that you can have a discussion about whether the rule is true or false.

4 Continue until everyone has had a chance to run to one of the chairs.

Follow-up

You may find that there are things you need to revise if students make a lot of mistakes with the rules. For reference, here is a check of the 'false' language statements:

1 The comparative forms of longer adjectives don't end in -er.
2 Many nouns don't have a plural ending in -s. Men, women, children, feet, teeth for example.

3 You use *a* before words beginning with a consonant, or a consonant sound, e.g. *a university, a union*, which are pronounced with an initial /j/; you use *an* before words beginning with a vowel and some words where the initial consonant is silent, e.g. *heir*, pronounced /eə(r)/.

4 *Next to* and *near* do not mean the same thing. *Next to* means *beside*; *near* is less precise, meaning *close* but not stating precisely where.

5 Do not use *do* in questions with *can* and *must. Can you swim? Must we leave now?*

6 Do not use *too* before a noun, only before an adjective or adverb.

7 The past tense of *drive* is *drove*, and the past participle is *driven*.

Comments

1 If you like this activity but are worried that some of your weaker students are not capable of doing it, then you can dispense with the numbers. Tell them that anyone who thinks they know the answer can run to the chairs. This might sound like a recipe for chaos, but members of the same team are unlikely to compete with each other, and will stop if they see that someone else from the same team has a better chance of reaching the chair.

2 If, on the other hand, you are worried about the students colliding, you can have two chairs at each end of the room, so that they race for different chairs. However, I really recommend that you try it with just one. There may be some collisions, but it is much more memorable.

3 This activity is set at Intermediate +, because explaining language rules is quite a complex thing to do for students, even if the rules themselves are quite elementary.

Variation

A less energetic and kinaesthetic version of this activity is what is usually referred to as a Grammar Auction. In this case, you write a series of sentences on the board, some of which are correct and some are not. You then divide the class into groups, and give them a theoretical amount of money, e.g. a thousand pounds. They then read the list of sentences, knowing that some of them may be wrong. They decide which ones they think are right. Then the teacher offers the sentences one by one for auction. If any of the groups think the sentence is correct, they can bid for it. The teacher continues until the bidding stops. Students should be constantly reminded that they only have a limited amount of money and they may want to bid for other sentences.

Again, this fun activity is a way of revising what you think the students should know. If they make mistakes on the incorrect sentences, you may need to do extra revision. However, it is also a good opportunity for peer teaching. If some groups think that a sentence is correct and others think it is wrong, then they can learn something from each other.

3.7 Charades

Level   Intermediate +

Time   15 minutes +

Aims   To use mime to elicit names of films, television shows, etc.

Charades is a game where people mime the names of films, television shows, book titles, or pop songs and other people have to guess the name from the mime. It is a traditional party game in many English-speaking countries, and some of the conventions that apply when native English speakers play it are listed below. If the game is played in your country too, then you may prefer to use local conventions. It works best with a maximum of about 16 students.

Preparation

You need two cardboard boxes or other containers. Explain to the students that they are going to mime the titles of films, television shows, books, and songs. Before you start, you have to agree on certain conventions. If the game is well known in your country, you can simply use the conventions that everyone knows. If the game is not well known, or if you want to show the class how English-speaking people play it, teach them the following mime conventions:

1   Indicate a book title by putting your hands together as if you are praying, then unfold them.

2   Indicate a film title by making an 'O' shape with one hand and making a circular motion with the other hand as if you are operating an old-fashioned movie camera.

3   Indicate a television show by miming a box shape.

4   Indicate the name of a song by opening and closing your mouth like a fish!

5   Hold up fingers to indicate the number of words in the title. Then indicate which word you are going to mime first by pointing to the finger which represents that word. For example, if the title is *Lord of the Rings*, and you want to start by miming *Rings*, you hold up four fingers, and then point to the fourth finger.

6   When you have indicated which word you are going to mime, show how many syllables there are in the word by holding the correct number of fingers against your arm. If for any reason you are going to mime just one syllable, then indicate which syllable with the fingers still against your arm. For example, if you want to mime the word *Superman*, but you want to mime *man* first, show the three fingers against your arm, then point to the third one.

You may want to encourage the class to think about miming just one syllable, and they can choose the syllable by sound. So you could mime *Superman* by pointing at the first syllable, and then miming *soup*! Explain to students that this is a very useful strategy when trying to mime abstract things. For example, to mime the word *understand*, it might be easiest to simply mime *under* and *stand*.

7 Indicate whether words are long or short by holding your hands close together or far apart. Imagine someone who has just caught a fish showing how long it is!

8 Confirm that your partners have guessed a word correctly by tapping your index finger on your nose and pointing to the person who made the correct guess. (Nose = knows. This is very English!)

9 In English, we say that someone is 'warm' if they are getting close to guessing something, and 'cold' if they are not close. You can, if you wish, incorporate these conventions into the activity. The conventional way of indicating 'getting warm' is to pull a single finger across your forehead as if you are wiping the sweat away. To indicate 'cold', hold your elbows and shiver. In fact, people usually just nod and smile if the answer is getting warm, and shake their head if it is not.

Procedure

1 Put the class into two teams, Team A and Team B. Ask each team to confer quietly and write titles of books, television shows, movies, or pop songs on individual pieces of paper. They should write at least enough for everyone in the opposite team to have a chance to mime something. They then put the pieces of paper in one of the containers. Each container must contain only pieces of paper from one team.

2 Invite someone from Team A to take a piece of paper from Team B's container. Note that this person will mime the title to his/her own team.

3 Ask the student to use the conventions listed above, or equivalent local conventions. The rest of the team should call out to indicate that they understand.

Examples *Person miming opens and closes mouth like a fish.*
Rest of team: Song title!

Person miming holds up four fingers.
Rest of team: Four words!

Person miming points at third finger.
Rest of team: Third word!

Person miming holds two fingers against arm.
Rest of team: Two syllables! etc.

4 The student then mimes the title. When the team get the answer, Team B chooses a title from Team A's container.

5 If you like, you can put a time-limit on each mime to add excitement. The team gets a point only if they get the mime in a particular period of time. Five minutes should be enough.

Follow-up

Write the titles of the films, books, etc. that have been mimed on the board. Ask people to indicate which films they have seen, books they have read, etc. For homework, ask them to write a review or synopsis of one of them.

3.8 Hot seat

There are several versions of this activity. It is suitable for all levels; however, it works best with Intermediate classes and above, as lower-level students may become frustrated if they are unable to think quickly enough.

Level Intermediate +

Time 15 minutes

Aims To encourage students to think quickly, give opinions, and express contrasting views.

Preparation

Place one or two chairs at the front of the class depending on whether you are doing the main version of the activity or the variation.

Procedure

1 Elicit a series of topics that one can have contrasting views about and write them on the board. They should be things that a student can say: *I like/don't like ...* or *I think X is good/bad/right/wrong*, etc.

2 If the students seem unable to think of any, here are some inoffensive possibilities that you can start with.

Examples *a particular colour (e.g. red) for clothing*
Italian (or some other) food
a particular sport
a particular singer or band
a particular pastime, e.g. watching television

3 If you want to deal with more serious subjects, and you think your students can deal with them linguistically, here are some suggestions.

Examples *global warming*
old people

crime in your city
the government
violent computer games

4   When there are 8–10 topics on the board, ask for two volunteers. One should sit on the chair (Student A) and the other (Student B) should stand behind the chair. Explain that Student A is going to give his/her opinion about one of the topics on the board, but at a certain point, Student B is going to clap his/her hands, and then Student A has to express an opinion which is completely the opposite.

5   Now ask the rest of the class to ask Student A a question about one of the topics. The question should elicit an opinion or ask about a like or dislike.

Examples   *Do you like Italian food?*
What do you think about (name of local band)?
What do you think about the government?

6   The student starts to speak, giving a view on the subject. He/she must say something positive or negative, not simply *I don't have an opinion about that.*

7   At a certain point, Student B claps his/her hands. Immediately Student A must change his/her opinion and try to say something that is the complete opposite of what he/she started out saying. Student B can clap hands two or three times, and Student A has to change every time.

8   Put a time limit of five minutes on this. Invite another two students to take part.

Variation

You can do the same thing with two students sitting in front of the class. If there are two, they must argue against each other. So, for example, if the question is: *What do you think about (name of local band)?* if the first person says they like the band, the second student MUST disagree. And when the other student claps his/her hands, they must swap opinions.

This sounds complicated and chaotic, but it is remarkable how well students can do this if they concentrate.

Follow-up

For homework, ask students to write a conversation giving two contrasting opinions about one of the subjects which was covered in the activity.

4

Drama club

This chapter is called 'Drama club' because the activities here are designed for teachers who want to organize an extra-curricular activity which involves English.

The first seven activities are therefore designed as warm-up activities, some of them quite physical, and many of them require little English, so they should be manageable with a group of enthusiastic but mixed ability students. Apart from their warm-up value, they are also designed to help the students realize that this is not a normal English class, and the usual classroom rules and relationships need not apply.

The remaining eight activities require greater ability with English; students are encouraged to improvise and 'think on their feet'. Many students may want to join a drama group because they like the atmosphere, but may also worry that their English is not good enough. For this reason, there are notes that indicate parts which can be played by students who may be good at acting, mime, comedy, etc., but are less confident in expressing themselves in English.

Time and space are important considerations. Some of the activities may take longer than you can afford in the context of a normal English lesson and, more importantly, most of them require an open space for the work. You may also want to advise students who attend these sessions to wear loose comfortable clothes, and girls should definitely not wear high-heeled shoes.

Some of the activities refer to the 'team leader', who makes certain decisions about what happens. To begin with, the team leader will probably be the teacher. However, when the group has met a few times, people will understand how things work and you can invite someone else to be team leader.

The *Follow-up* suggestions in this section generally relate to classroom use of the activities. If students are attending a drama club activity, they will not usually have written work or other homework unless it is something they have to do before the next meeting of the group.

Generally speaking, these extra-curricular activities blur the distinction between teacher and students. They also require a higher level of student autonomy than the ones which are classroom-based. Some of the activities may require you to give some personal details about yourself, or generally behave in a more egalitarian way with your students than you may otherwise do in class. If you think the activity requires you to give too much information about yourself, you may prefer not to do it.

All the activities can also be used in the classroom, if you think you have the time and the right space for them.

4.1 Door window

Level Elementary +

Time 5 minutes

Aims To practise names of objects. To energize the group.

Preparation

No preparation is needed for this activity.

Procedure

1 Ask the students to stand in a crowd in front of you. Point to five or six things round the room and ask them to shout the English words for them back to you. The five or six words could be *door, window, chair, table, floor, ceiling*. Ask the class to shout them as loud as they can. Point at each of the items five or six times, in different sequences.

2 Now tell them that you are going to point at the same things again, but this time, they must shout out the wrong word. In other words, if you point at the door, they must not shout *door*, but they can shout *window, chair, table, floor,* or *ceiling*. They must not shout any other words.

This activity wakens the sleepiest class up, and is suitable for those with limited English, including beginners.

4.2 Move over if ...

Level   Elementary +

Time   10 minutes

Aims   To practise present and past tenses. To get the class warmed up mentally and physically.

Preparation

The students must have space to stand in a circle.

Procedure

1 The students stand in a circle, with one person in the middle. The object of the game is for the person in the middle to find a place in the circle, by asking some of the others to move. He/she says *Move over if ...* and completes the instruction.

Examples   *Move over if ...*
... you're wearing white socks/earrings.
... you have/have got black hair/a dog.
... you like pizza/football.
... you ate cheese today/watched television last night.

2 If, for example, the person in the middle says *Move over if you're wearing white socks*, and there are five students in the circle who are wearing white socks, these five students must run from their position in the circle and find another position. Meanwhile, the person who was in the middle runs to one of the places in the circle which has been vacated. Four of the five students who move will also find a recently vacated space in the circle. This leaves another student in the middle.

3 Continue until the class is really energized and warmed up.

Follow-up

Many students make elementary mistakes of grammar and collocation when they do this activity. A common example is *Move over if you wear trainers*, when they actually mean *... if you are wearing trainers*. If you do this as a classroom activity, you may wish to revise some of the things that need some attention.

Comments

Some teachers query the likelihood of someone being left in the middle of the circle when everyone has moved, on the grounds that the circle can always be made a little wider to accommodate an extra person. They think that chairs are better. Personally, I have never had a problem with people standing in a circle for this activity. In fact, students moving at high speed towards the same chair can be dangerous.

4.3 123–BANG!

Level Elementary +

Time 10 minutes

Aims To practise numbers with a simple warmer.

Preparation

Students must have space to stand in a circle.

Procedure

1 Students stand in a circle. You can be part of the circle, if you like. Explain that the aim is to count to a hundred, but when you reach the number 4, or a multiple of 4 (8, 12, etc.), or a number with 4 in it (14, 34, 41, etc.), you don't say the number, you say BANG! At first, tell the class that anyone who makes a mistake is 'out' (i.e. out of the game—but you will modify this later).

2 Start counting round the circle. When someone makes the first mistake (usually when the count reaches 8 or 12), you can ask the rest of the circle if he or she can have another chance. They will usually say *yes!*

3 Start the count again; the person after the one who made the mistake starts at 1 again. Allow two or three mistakes, then say, *OK, let's try to reach 100.* You can if you wish make people leave the circle if they make a mistake, but I think this breaks the class up, rather than taking the chance to bond them.

4 It will soon become clear that 100 is an unrealistic target. Every time there is a mistake after the first practice sessions, reduce the target by 10, until it is down to 40. This means that the game can end on a BANG! and avoids the difficulty of doing all the 40s as BANGS!

Variation

Most students find this version of the game demanding enough, but if they do it really well, then there is an even more challenging version called WHIZZ–BANG! In this version, students say BANG! instead of numbers related to 4, as above, but they also say WHIZZ! for numbers related to 7. When numbers are related to both 4 and 7, (14 or 28 for example), they say WHIZZ–BANG!

Follow-up

If you do this as a classroom activity, you may feel the need to do some further practice with numbers if students have real problems with sequencing of numbers or pronunciation.

4.4 Duck chicken

Level Elementary +

Time 5 minutes

Aims To understand and react spontaneously to a prompt. To energize the class.

Preparation

The students must have space to stand in a circle. It is very important that students wear shoes which are suitable for running. If you as the teacher want to take part in this, you need to be quite fit.

Procedure

The whole class stand in a circle. Nominate one student, who will leave the circle and walk around the outside, tapping the people he or she passes and saying *Duck*. At a certain point, he or she touches someone and says *Chicken!* and begins to run round the circle to get back to his or her original position (which must still be a vacant place in the circle). The 'chicken' student chases the original student round the circle. If the original student makes it back to his or her original place in the circle, then the chicken student continues the process. If the original student is caught on the way back to the vacant spot, he or she must go round again.

Comments

Some teachers feel uncomfortable about doing this with a group where some students are fitter than others. In my experience, having done this activity with groups as young as ten and others who were senior citizens, as well as groups where some people were clearly fitter than others, everyone enjoys it.

4.5 Murder

Level Elementary +

Time 5–10 minutes

Aims To bond and build up trust in the class.

Preparation

Students must have an open space to work in. It is important that they have no qualms about touching each other. They are going to walk around with their eyes closed, so you need to appoint four monitors, who will not take part in the activity. The monitors must make sure that no one bumps into the furniture.

Procedure

1 Tell the class that they are going to walk around slowly with their eyes closed. Tell them that, after a few seconds, you are going to tap one of them on the shoulder once. This person is now the murderer, and will then try to murder everyone else in the class. Explain that the murderer, when he or she is chosen, murders the others by tapping them twice on the shoulder. This will distinguish the act of murder from the original tap, when you chose the murderer.

2 Explain also that when participants are murdered, they must scream. They can then open their eyes and become part of the monitoring force. Eventually, the murderer will be stalking just one or two people, while everyone watches.

Follow-up

Again, the main aim is group bonding and enjoyment, but students often like to discuss what they saw when they watched the remaining participants warily avoiding the murderer.

Comments

Safety is important in trust activities, especially when people have their eyes closed. Please make sure that at least four people are monitoring. The monitors should gently guide people away from furniture and other hazards.

4.6 The Hanging Gardens of Babylon

Level Elementary +

Time 15–20 minutes

Aims To practise paying close attention to instructions. To encourage students to sing, dance, mime, and express themselves without inhibition.

Preparation

Students must have space to stand in a circle. You may also want
pictures of a Viking, a palm tree, and a ballet dancer. Although the
name of the activity has merely been chosen for the length of the
phrase, you can if you wish give the class the following information
about the Hanging Gardens of Babylon:

*The Hanging Gardens of Babylon were one of the original Seven Wonders of
the World, a beautiful set of gardens situated in what is now Iraq. They were
built by King Nebuchadnezzar the Second for his wife Amytis of Media, who
loved trees and beautiful plants. They were destroyed by an earthquake about
2,100 years ago.*

Procedure

1 Students stand in a circle. You stand in the middle of the circle and
   give the following instruction.

   *This game is called The Hanging Gardens of Babylon. If I point at you and say
   'Hanging Gardens of Babylon', you must say 'Babylon' before I finish speaking.
   Let's practise that.*

2 Let lots of students practise this, then give this instruction.

   *Very good. Now it gets more difficult. If I ONLY say 'Babylon', you mustn't say
   anything at all. Let's practise that.*

3 Now point at different students, giving one or other of the two prompts. When one of them makes a mistake (usually by saying *Babylon* when you have only said *Babylon*), then he or she comes into the centre of the circle and shouts one of the two prompts until another student makes a mistake.

4 Now make the activity more challenging. You are going to give them three new prompts, and these prompts are *Viking*, *palm tree*, and *ballet dancer*. Make sure that the students understand the meaning of all of these things. If necessary, show them pictures.

5 The next three sets of instructions are a little complicated. Each of the instructions will require three people to respond. Explain the following rules:

a When you point at someone and say *Viking*, the person you point at has to make a Viking helmet with his or her hands. Meanwhile, the people to the left and right of the Viking have to mime rowing the Viking boat, and make the sound of the sea whooshing past. Their oars must be outside the boat. If they row inside the boat, this is a mistake. Anyone who makes a mistake has to go to the middle of the circle.

b When you point at someone and say *palm tree*, the person you point at has to become a palm tree, swaying in the breeze. Meanwhile, the people on either side must become Hawaiian dancers, dancing away from the tree. While they dance, they have to sing a Hawaiian song (or what they think sounds like a Hawaiian song). If they don't sing, or if they dance towards the tree, this is a mistake, and they go into the middle of the circle.

c When you point at someone and say *ballet dancer*, the person you point at holds his or her hands like a ballet dancer, so that the people on either side can do a ballet pirouette, whilst humming a ballet tune (e.g. *Dance of the Sugar Plum Fairy* from Tchaikovsky's *Nutcracker Suite* which is easy and memorable).

6 Continue until everyone is energized and warmed up.

To recap: whoever is in the middle of the circle has to point at an individual in the circle and give one of the following prompts:

Hanging Gardens of Babylon
Babylon
Viking
palm tree
ballet dancer

Comments

It is possible that two or even three people will 'make a mistake' in their mimes. This is not a problem. You can either choose one of them to go to middle of the circle or let two or three of them give the instructions.

4.7 What time is it?

Level Elementary +

Time 15 minutes

Aims To practise intonation in order to convey emotion. To energize the class.

Preparation

No preparation is needed for this activity.

Procedure

1 Choose five students from the class and ask them to stand in a line.

2 Tell the first student (Student A) in the line to ask the question *What time is it?* to Student B *angrily*. Let Student A practise asking the question angrily. Ask the rest of the class if they sound angry enough.

3 Now tell Student B to reply angrily with one word: *What?* He or she should use rising intonation to indicate that he or she didn't hear the first time. Let Student A and Student B practise the two lines.

4 Now ask Student A to repeat the question *What time is it?* This time Student B says *I don't know!* Student A finishes the exchange by indicating Student C and saying: *Well, ask him/her!*

So, the complete dialogue is as follows:

Student A: What time it is?
Student B: What?
Student A: What time is it?
Student B: I don't know!
Student A: Well, ask him/her!
Student B: What time is it?
Student C: What? etc.

5 Now the team is ready to try the dialogue all the way down the line: Student A to Student B, B to C, etc.

6 When Student D asks Student E, and Student E says: *I don't know!* stop the action and tell Student E that he or she DOES know. Tell Student E to tell Student D the time calmly. *It's half past ten* (or whatever the time is).

7 Now tell Student D to thank Student E profusely, but only using the words *Thank you.* Tell him or her to make the *Thank you* as emphatic as possible.

8 Student D now tells Student C the time calmly, and Student C gives a big *Thank you.* Continue until Student B tells Student A.

9 Now repeat the whole exercise, letting Student E start.

10 The five members of the first team then choose five more people to stand in a line.

11 Ask the class to give you a new question. Use the new question with the new team.

12 Continue until everyone in the class has had a chance to play.

Comments

When you ask the group to give you a new question for the second or subsequent groups, they may not offer one which 'works'. It doesn't matter; accept whatever they say and let the second and subsequent groups try to make it work. For example, if they offer *What's your name?*, don't reject it—let the team try it:

Example *Student A: What's your name?*
Student B: What?
Student A: What's your name?
Student B: I don't know!
Student A: Well, ask her!

They will soon realize that questions which ask for more general information are the ones which will work.

4.8 Party guests

Level Intermediate +

Time 15–20 minutes

Aims To create a scene where one character has to guess who all the other characters are.

Preparation

It must be possible for two characters to leave the room and not hear what is going on with the rest of the class.

Procedure

1 Explain what is going to happen. Two characters are going to host a party. Three other characters are going to be their party guests. The guests are going to have a characteristic or peculiarity of some kind, which the hosts have to guess. This characteristic can relate to their work, for example, or could be a speech habit.

2 Choose the two party hosts and ask them to leave the room. Explain that when they come back, the three guests who have some particular characteristic will arrive one by one.

3 Choose the three party guests. With the help of the rest of the class, choose a recognizable characteristic that they can indicate in their behaviour. Here is a list to help you start, but please encourage the class to choose their own.

Examples *an opera singer who never stops singing or a ballet dancer who never
stops dancing*
*someone who is obsessed with cleanliness, and keeps cleaning everything,
including the glass of wine given to them by the host*
someone who repeats everything that they hear
someone who thinks he is Sherlock Holmes

You can see that many of these parts can be played by students who are not so confident about their English, but who have good musical or mime skills.

4 Let the three guests practise how they will indicate their peculiarity or characteristic. Then ask them to leave the room and ask them to send in the two hosts. Tell the guests to come in one at a time. The first guest should come in as soon as the activity starts. The second guest should enter two minutes later and the third guest two minutes after that. It is not necessary for the hosts to guess what the first guest is doing before the second and third guests arrive.

5 Ask the two hosts to start preparing food and drink for their party. Very soon, there will be a knock at the door and their first guest will arrive. Ask the hosts to welcome the guest and give them a drink. The guest should start indicating their characteristic as soon as they arrive.

6 The guests should arrive at two minute intervals, regardless of whether the hosts have worked out what the previous guests are doing.

7 The hosts engage their three guests in 'normal' party conversation, and try to work out their characteristics. When they think they know, they can ask a direct question: *Are you an opera singer? Do you think you are Sherlock Holmes? Do you repeat what people say?* The rest of the class can help the host by applauding successful guesses or near misses.

8 Continue until the hosts have worked out all three peculiarities.

Variation

You can if you wish have more than two hosts and more than three guests. You may find that if there are more guests it can get a little complicated and untidy. Also, this activity is a lot of fun to watch, so the rest of the class can enjoy it even if they are not involved. This game is based on a television programme in which there is only one host.

Follow-up

If you are doing this as a classroom activity, the class can write what happened as a story for homework.

4.9 Foreign expert

Level Intermediate +

Time 15–30 minutes

Aims To practise translation and interpreting skills. To practise reported speech.

Preparation

No preparation is needed for this activity.

Procedure

1 Explain to the students that they are going to work in pairs. One of the pair is going to be an expert on a particular subject, but the expert doesn't speak English at all. The other is an interpreter. The country that the expert is from and the language should be inventions, not real ones.

2 Tell the pairs to work together for a few minutes. They should decide on the expert's invented nationality and what his or her expertise is. They should also practise speaking in the invented language. Both members of the pair are going to have to speak it.

3 Invite one of the pairs to the front of the class and ask them to explain who they are. The expert, who cannot speak English, can't say anything at this point. The interpreter says something like this: *I'd like to introduce Professor Zog, who comes from Bonkoland. He's an expert on birds but I'm afraid he only speaks Bonko. But if you have some questions for him, I can translate them for him.*

4 The rest of the class now ask Professor Zog questions about birds. The interpreter then translates the questions into Bonko and Professor Zog answers in Bonko. The translator then translates the answers into English.

5 Continue until as many pairs as you wish have had a chance to do this.

Variation

If you like, you can ask the class to write a subject for the experts on a piece of paper. The pieces of paper are then put in a box. The pairs work on their language skills, then come to the front of the class and take a piece of paper from the box. It is only now that they find out what they are experts about.

Follow-up

Ask the class to write down the questions and answers that they remember. They may only remember one from each of the experts. This is a good way to practise reported speech.

Example   *Luis asked Professor Zog which was his favourite bird, and Professor Zog said that he liked parrots.*

Comments

1 Encourage the experts to use gesture and mime as much as possible in their answers. This way, the students can get an idea of what to expect in the translation.

2 The role of expert is perfect for students who are less proficient in English but good at mime.

4.10 A day in the life

Level   Intermediate +

Time   15–30 minutes

Aims   To practise past tenses in a dramatic context. To listen to and act out an incident from someone's life.

Preparation

In this activity, students are invited to talk about an incident in their life, which involved about four or five other people, and then watch the incident acted out by other members of the class. The activity works best if the incident was something amusing. Students may feel so comfortable with the group that they are happy to relive a serious or traumatic incident in their life, but you should not suggest they do this; it should only happen if the students offer to tell the story.

It is a good idea to tell students that you are planning to do this activity beforehand, for example during the previous session, to give them time to think of a suitable story. If you like, you can start with a simple amusing incident from your own life.

Procedure

1   Having given the students time to think about their stories, preferably by telling them about this activity in advance, ask for a volunteer to tell his or her story.

2   Give the rest of the class a chance to ask for details, if they want.

3   With the whole class, identify the main characters who will feature in the story. The storyteller should have the final decision about this, but other members of the group can make suggestions.

4   Either ask the storyteller to indicate whom he or she would like to play the parts (preferred option), or ask for volunteers from the class.

5   Ask the volunteers to act out the different scenes from the story.

6   Ask the storyteller, and the rest of the class, to comment on the performance. Ask them to be positive but also to point out any discrepancies or omissions from the original story.

7   Let the whole class make suggestions for changes and improvements. Then ask the characters to act it out again.

Follow-up

If you do this as a class activity, ask the class to write the incident as a narrative for homework.

Variation

The following variation is good if you have a large drama group or class. If the activity is a success, and you want to do it again, divide the class into groups of four or five. Ask them to work separately on a life story, and then invite one or more of the groups to act it out. In this case, of course, the other students will not have been part of the practice process, so the only person who can comment on the performance is the person whose story it is. However, the rest of the larger group should indicate what they think of the performance.

Comments

I first did this activity with a group of students who were attending a summer school drama workshop. They were students I had only known for three or four days. I told them about something that happened to me when I was 14 years old. I was watching Manchester United football team play away from home. I was standing behind the goal with some friends. Next to us, there was a big muscular Manchester United fan.

Before the match started, he blew up a red balloon and gave it to me. 'Go and put this on the penalty spot,' he said, rather aggressively. I laughed, but he clearly expected me to do this. So I took the balloon, went over the wall and walked to the penalty spot. I put the balloon on the penalty spot, kicked it and—miraculously—it floated into the net. About six thousand Manchester United fans roared with approval. However, I was breaking the rules of the stadium, and two stewards came and marched me away. I found myself in the area reserved for hooligans, and guarded by the police.

Fortunately, the police officer who spoke to me was an understanding person. He could see that I wasn't a hooligan and he believed me when I told him that I had felt threatened by the man who blew up the balloon. 'I should throw you out of the ground,' he said, 'but I won't do that. But I can't let you go back to the place where you were, so you will have to watch the game from the police camera room.' So that's what happened. I was at a live soccer match, but I had to watch it on television, surrounded by some very amusing police officers!

4.11 Trip to America

Level Intermediate +

Time 15 minutes

Aims To practise the language of comparisons.

This activity is based on the more famous Balloon Game, in which three people are in a sinking hot air balloon. The only way to stop the balloon crashing is for one of them to jump out. The three have to explain why they should remain in the balloon and why one (or both) of the others should throw themselves out.

This is a rather macabre activity; the following is a less morbid version of the game. In this version, the local authority of your town has decided to send five key workers on an all-expenses-paid visit to New York. However, do not tell the class about this at first. Just tell them that they have to choose an occupation, the kind of job that is essential to the successful running of a city.

You can if you wish change the destination to somewhere that you think your students may find more exciting, like Las Vegas or Rio de Janeiro.

Preparation

If you have the technology, prepare a slide show of images of the place where the all-expenses-paid trip is going. You can easily download some pictures from a search engine. Check that you are allowed to use the images in the classroom; there may be copyright issues even if you are not planning to use them commercially.

Procedure

1 Ask the students to write down an occupation on a piece of paper, with their name next to it. The occupation should be one which does essential work for a local authority.

2 Collect the papers in and write the occupations on the board. If there are two the same, toss a coin, and the loser has to think of a new occupation.

Example Sergio   *doctor*
Luisa   *nurse*
Toni   *traffic police officer*
Jo   *road cleaner*
and so on

3 Now explain that the local authority of the place where you live has decided to send a number of essential workers on an all-expenses-paid visit to New York City (or any city of your choice which is likely to appeal to students as somewhere glamorous). The number should be five, or fewer if there are only five people in the group.

4 Tell everyone in the group to vote for themselves plus four other essential workers to have the free holiday. Ask them to write their votes on a piece of paper, and to put the pieces of paper in a cardboard box. Ask two students to count the votes. One of them reads out what people have written on their pieces of paper, the other adds the votes on the board.

Example Sergio   *doctor* ✓✓✓
Luisa   *nurse* ✓✓✓✓✓
Toni   *traffic police officer* ✓
Jo   *road cleaner* ✓✓✓

5 You can now announce that, at this stage, the students with the highest number of votes are Students A, B, C, D, and E. However, you understand that some workers may feel that they deserve the holiday more. Therefore, allow the workers who were not chosen to talk about why they think they deserve the holiday, and which other worker they think they should replace.

6 When the ones who did not win the holiday have had their chance to support their own right for a holiday, the ones who have the holiday have the right of reply.

7 When everyone has had a chance to speak, have another vote. Ask everyone to do the same thing again, voting for themselves and four other people. The pieces of paper go into the box and two students count the votes. Choose a different pair of students do it this time. This time, the votes will probably change.

Example
Sergio   doctor ✓
Luisa   nurse ✓✓✓
Toni   traffic police officer ✓
Jo   road cleaner ✓✓✓✓✓✓✓✓

8 Announce the winners of the five free holidays in New York City.

4.12 The big question

Level Upper-intermediate +

Time 15–30 minutes

Aims To improvise a debate where participants are given a line they have to incorporate into a discussion.

Preparation

You need volunteers who are prepared to have a discussion about a topic they have not prepared, and into which they have to incorporate a line they have been given.

Procedure

1 Explain that you need four volunteers. Tell them that they are going to leave the room for a few minutes, and when they come back, you are going to give each of them a piece of paper with a statement on it. They will have to find a way to incorporate the statement into a discussion about a subject that they have not prepared for. The discussion will be called 'The big question'.

2 Ask the four volunteers to leave the room for five minutes. Hereafter, these four are referred to as 'the principal speakers'.

3 While they are outside the room, tell the rest of the class what is written on the four pieces of paper. Here are four statements you could use in this activity:

Examples
My uncle grows his own tobacco.
There are more than ten thousand lakes in Canada.
My ambition is to learn to fly a plane.
Whales can communicate with each other.

4 When the rest of the class know what the statements are, ask them to suggest the 'big question', a topic for debate. They should try to choose something which is completely different from all the statements. Suggestions for the topic of debate might include the following:

Examples
How can you be a success in life?
What's the best way to find a life partner?
Is physical exercise important?

What's the point of studying?
Which person has had the biggest influence on our lives in this country?

5   Ask for a volunteer to chair the debate.

6   The principal speakers come back into the classroom and sit at a table at the front of the room ready for the debate. Give each of them a piece of paper containing the statement they will eventually have to incorporate into the story.

7   The chair sits in the middle and announces the subject. *Good evening and welcome to The Big Question. Tonight's big question is: How can you be a success in life? I'd like to start by asking (Student A) to give his/her thoughts on this important subject.*

8   Before they start speaking, tell the four that they are not allowed to use their statement in their opening remarks.

9   Each of the principal speakers makes a short statement about the *big question*. Then the chair invites them to comment on what each other has said. At this point, they can try to steer the conversation towards their own line. This part is extremely amusing for the watching group, but please warn them not to cheer or applaud if the statement is said.

10 Open the discussion to the whole class, and invite questions to the principal speakers.

11 Continue the discussion until all four speakers have managed to say their statement.

12 Ask the principal speakers if they can work out what the others had to say.

Variation

You can if you wish choose not to tell the rest of the class what is written on the pieces of paper. When you have heard all four statements, you can stop the debate, and ask the rest of the class if they have any idea what the four statements were. This is an interesting way to do it, the only disadvantage being that the students don't have the opportunity to choose a 'big question' that is different from the statements.

4.13 Change emotions

Level Upper-intermediate +

Time 15 minutes

Aims To practise expressing emotions.

Preparation

You need three boxes for this activity.

Procedure

1   Tell the class that you are going to ask for two volunteers to devise a conversation about a particular subject. Allow everyone to listen to all the instructions before they volunteer.

2 Ask everyone in the class to write an occupation on a piece of paper. Put the pieces of paper in the first box.

3 Now ask everyone to write down a conversation topic and put it in the second box.

4 Finally, ask them to write down an adjective (or an adverb) which could be used to describe the way people talk. Give them *angrily* as an example. These papers go in the third box.

5 Now ask for two volunteers. First of all, they each take a piece of paper out of the first box which gives them an occupation. They tell the rest of the class what their occupation is, e.g. *doctor* and *window cleaner*.

6 Now a third volunteer (the reader) picks a topic of conversation from the second box, e.g. *sport*. The two original volunteers start a conversation about sport. They have to talk about the subject in the style of the occupation. For example, the doctor can talk about sports injuries he or she has treated.

7 After three or four minutes, the team leader says *Change emotions*. The reader takes a piece of paper out of the third box with a new emotion, e.g. *excited*. The two people must continue their conversation in an excited way. The team leader says *Change emotions* two more times, and finally *Thirty seconds to complete*.

Variation

There are various ways you can modify this activity, to make it more dramatic, or to make it easier for the two participants. For example, you can invite another student to join the original two at any time. The third student takes another occupation from the box, tells the class what he or she is, and takes part in the conversation.

Another variation is that both the participants, or all three, can take part in the conversation using different emotions. They all select an emotion at the beginning of the activity, and when the team leader shouts *Change emotions*, they all choose a new one, or exchange the ones that they have.

Comments

1 The role of the reader is a good one for one of the weaker or less confident students in the class.

2 Some students feel more comfortable if they are allowed to sit down during activities like this one. You may want to start with two chairs at the front of the class. If a third character enters the action, they can bring a chair with them to join the other two.

4.14 Reporters

Level Upper-intermediate +

Time 15–20 minutes

Aims To sharpen listening and note-taking skills. To practise reported speech.

Preparation

You need a video/DVD player and a video/DVD of a movie or a documentary, where there are a lot of narrative events that can be described. You only need to show about five minutes. An action movie would be good for this, and the opening section of a James Bond movie would be very good. You need between six and ten volunteers.

Procedure

1 Put the volunteers in two equal teams, three, four, or five in each team. The two teams stand facing each other in front of a television. One team faces away from the screen, the other team faces them, in a position so that they can see the screen. The team which cannot see the television should have a pen and notebook. The rest of the class should also be able to see the screen.

2 Play the video or DVD, without sound. Tell the people who can see the TV to describe the action. The other team must take notes. If you like, you can give them two chances to do this. Remember that the sequence should be no more than five minutes long.

3 When the sequence has finished, ask everyone to sit down. Then invite one of the note-takers to stand up and explain what was described. The rest of the class should make notes about anything that he or she missed or described inaccurately.

4 Invite another of the note-takers to stand up and say what was described. Again, the rest of the class should make notes about the accuracy of what was said.

At this stage, it doesn't matter whether the action is being described in the present or past tense. However, it is probable that there will be items of vocabulary that the students need to complete their descriptions. Discuss the words that they need, and write them on the board.

5 When you have listened to two or three of the descriptions, tell the class to think about how a news reporter would describe the events. Would he or she use different language? Divide the participants into as many groups as there were original reporters, and give them time to work on changing it into a news report. Suggest that everybody in the group should take part in some way. Two people can be in the studio, one can be a roving reporter, and any others can be participants in the scene or witnesses.

6 Invite one or more of the groups to act out their television news report.

Follow-up

If you are doing this in class, ask the students to write the final version of the news story as a newspaper report for homework.

Acknowledgements

This is an adaptation of an activity I saw at a conference in Romania. I would like to thank two excellent teachers, Mirela Ionescu and Monica Mondiru, for their permission to use it.

4.15 Television news

Level   Upper-intermediate +

Time   60 minutes

Aims   To practise planning, interviewing, and reporting in the context of devising and filming a news programme.

Preparation

The class is going to devise and film a news programme. You need a video/DVD camera for this activity. You also need a table and two chairs, which will be the news studio. You may want to produce some kind of backdrop to make this look authentic. A map of the world is colourful and successful from this point of view. Depending on the stories that emerge, you may need some props and costumes. If you are planning to make the film in a school, try to get access to as many parts of the school as possible, e.g. the kitchen or the sports gymnasium. It is also helpful if you have access to some safe outdoor locations for the filming. School sports fields are very good. Do not encourage the students to set their story in a busy street; filming in the street is disruptive and can be dangerous.

If there is someone in the class who has some experience of making video films, ask him or her to be the camera operator. Otherwise you, the teacher, should do it. Read the notes at the end of this activity for tips about filming.

Procedure

1 Explain to the class that you want them to devise a local news programme. You are going to divide them into groups of three or four (depending on the size of the class—it's best to have a maximum of six news items). Each of these groups is going to devise a five-minute piece about some local news.

2 In addition, you have to choose two people who are going to read the news. It is best if the class vote for these people. Explain to the newsreaders that, during the preparation process, they have to visit the different groups to find out details of their news story. For this reason, it is very important that the groups liaise at all times with the newsreaders, and keep them informed where they are when they are practising.

3 Choose the topic. It is best to offer a series of possible news stories, and let the groups choose one. If there are groups who are not inspired by your list, they can think of their own subject. The following subjects work well.

Examples   *a local sportsman/woman or athlete who has done something good, e.g. won a medal or been picked for the national team*
a local person who is in the news for some (positive) reason, e.g. he or she has won a prize or something similar
a robbery at a local bank/shop
plans to build a new international airport in your town
an interview with the oldest person in the town, who has just reached his or her 90th, 100th, 105th birthday, etc.
the traffic and weather report

4 The different groups go away and discuss how they will present their news item. Ideally, one of the group is a reporter on location and the others are somehow involved in the item. For example, in the first news item suggestion above, if there are four people in the group, one person will be the reporter, one will be the sportsman or woman, one can be his or her trainer, and any other people can be members of the sportsperson's family.

5 Give the groups a maximum of 30 minutes to think about what they want to do. Ask the newsreaders to constantly monitor what is going on. Give a particular time when everyone must congregate for the filming.

6 Filming of the news programme can be done without editing in the following way:

a Choose the order of items.
b Film the newsreaders introducing the item: *Local athlete (X) has been chosen to represent our country at the Olympic Games. Over to (Y), who is with (X) now.*

c Stop the camera. Relocate for the filming of the first item.
d Film the first item. Stop the camera. Relocate back to the news studio and film the introduction to the next item, etc.

7 The marvellous thing about this activity is that the programme is ready to show as soon as you have filmed the last item, which should be the two newsreaders saying goodbye.

Follow-up

Discuss the film. Try to find something positive to say about everyone's performance. Ask students to say who they thought were the best performers. Ask them if they want to make any comments about their own performances.

Comments

1 Tell the groups that, as far as possible, the stories should be static. It is dangerous and difficult to do moving shots, particularly if the camera operator has to move backwards.

2 Although you plan to do this without editing, you can allow the groups one or two chances to stop and start again. You just need to rewind to the start of the section and begin again. But the news programme is not meant to be perfect, so only give them two chances to start again.

5
Working with scripts

'Scripts' refers to any long dialogue, sketch, or short play that you might want to use with your class or drama group. This chapter contains a set of eight original sketches and eight suggestions about how to use them. Each of the sketches is used to illustrate a different activity, but in fact the activities are interchangeable, and most of them will work with any piece that you want to use.

The accompanying activities include suggestions for language work—improvisation, prediction, and discussion, for example. This section is also an extension of Chapter 4 *Drama club* and the sketches can be rehearsed and performed, if that is your aim.

Each activity offers the students a chance to work with the material in different ways, for example discussing lines before you do the sketch, predicting content, working out endings of their own etc. Some of the activities will benefit from being treated as gapfill activities on first reading, and an indication is given of which words can be left out to show how the activity works. One activity suggests jumbling the lines of part of the sketch, and an example is given of how to do this.

The eight original sketch scripts are at the end of the chapter.

Some general points about using the sketches:

1 When you first work with one of the sketches, it is recommended that you divide the students into groups and let them take turns to do a *read-through*. Each group reads the sketch through two or three times, allowing everyone a chance to read at least one part. Students who are not participating in the read-through can listen and help others with their *delivery* (i.e. the way they say the lines). Non-speakers should listen without looking at the script, so that they can tell the readers if they are speaking the lines clearly enough.

2 Encourage the students to interpret the sketches in any way they wish, using different emotions, gestures, etc. It is important that they feel that they are making the sketch their own. Whatever the sex of the characters in the sketches, they can be played by male or female students. Most of the characters in most of the sketches can perform their parts standing up (more people can see what is happening this way).

3   Try not to impose any of your own ideas about 'acting'. There are only three rules for acting at this level:
    • remember where the audience is
    • make sure you can be heard
    • avoid the furniture.
    At the same time, if you like the idea of being a director, tell the student that you will give them advice about how to play the sketch if they ask you for it.

4   Some of the sketches are in two or three parts. You can, if you like, give the different parts to different groups to rehearse and perform. This way, the other students can watch the development of the sketch they have worked on.

5   There are three different versions of Sketch 8 *The restaurant*. There is an explanation of how the versions are different in the notes for Activity 5.8. Divide the class into three groups for this one and ask each group to provide a pair of actors to act out their version.

6   An obvious follow-up to using any sketch is to discuss, predict, and/ or improvise what happened next. Procedures for doing this are outlined in the *Follow-up* section of Activity 5.1, and this is referred to in the *Follow-up* notes of the other activities. Try to think of simple ways of working out what is happening or what is going to happen. For example, encourage the students to say: *I think she's waiting for a bus*, or *I think he's going to arrest the man*, rather than *She might be waiting for a bus*, or *He might be about to arrest the man*. If you keep it simple, people will feel confident about saying more.

7   Try to give the less proficient students in the group something to do. For example, in Sketch 4 *Bert and the bulldozer*, someone (preferably more than one person) needs to play the bulldozer. In Sketch 7 *Animal farm*, students can play other animals who are listening to the debate.

8   If you want the students to perform the sketches in front of an audience, then the characters should learn their parts. If you simply want the class/group to perform the sketches to each other, they can do this holding the script.

Notes about terminology

1   You probably know the noun *cast*, meaning 'the list of actors in a play or film'. *Cast* is also used in the activity instructions as a verb, as in 'ask the three groups to cast the sketch'. This instruction means that it's time for the students to decide which members of the group are actually going to perform the sketch.

2   The word *punchline* refers to the funny line at the end of a sketch. Mostly, these notes suggest telling the class not to worry about a punchline if they are devising their own alternative ending to the sketch, or devising a scene to show what happened next.

3   Activities involving *mime* do not assume that students will be able to mime like a professional artist, nor that mime should be silent. The normal definition of *mime* is 'a performance using gestures and body movements without words or other sounds', but students can ignore this and use as many sounds as they feel appropriate. For example, in Sketch 4 *Bert and the bulldozer,* students can play the part of the bulldozer, and this is usually quite noisy.

4   *Blocking* means working out where people are going to enter/leave the playing area, where they are going to stand or sit when they say their lines, where they are going to move and—very importantly— where the furniture is going to be. If different groups are working on the same material, and will act it out one after the other, it is important that they all agree on the position of the furniture.

5   As in Chapter 4, the procedure notes occasionally refer to the 'team leader'. The team leader will be responsible for starting certain activities (Activity 5.4 *Bert and the bulldozer,* for example). If the activity is taking place in the classroom, the team leader will probably be the teacher, although with drama group activities like this, it is recommended that the teacher should occasionally appoint one of the participants to be team leader.

6   *Tippex* is a noun/verb, the brand name of a substance that we use to 'white out' words or expressions. It is such a useful verb that it has entered the language in the same way as *Hoover* for vacuum cleaners. *Tippex out* is the normal form of the verb.

Final important note

The sketches can be adapted, and you have the author's permission to shorten or extend them, add characters and events, or change them in any way you choose. This does not apply to Sketch 8, however, which should be performed as written.

5.1 Noisy neighbours

Level   Elementary +

Time   15–30 minutes

Aims   To rehearse and perform a sketch in three parts.

Preparation

Photocopy Sketch 1 on page 108. Cut it into three parts.

Procedure

1 Divide the students into three groups. Give each group one part of the three-part sketch.

2 Ask them to rehearse their part of the sketch. Encourage different pairs to read the characters. If possible, find a way for the three groups to practise somewhere where they can't hear the other two groups.

3 Ask the three groups to *cast* the sketch, i.e. choose the two characters who are going to play the parts.

4 Act out the three parts of the sketch.

Follow-up

Discuss the performance. Ask the students how it felt not to know that the other groups were rehearsing.

With all the sketches, you can if you wish encourage the students to discuss and/or devise a scene to show what happened next. In the case of this sketch, they can either do it in their three groups, or do it all together. Encourage them to discuss what happened, but also to come up with lines that the characters might say. In the case of *Noisy neighbours*, they can if they wish bring the three characters together, and even add some more characters, to the final part of the sketch.

When they have discussed it for a while, put them back into smaller groups and ask them to improvise and rehearse the next scene. Again, this works better if the different groups can rehearse in separate rooms, although this may not be practical in some classroom situations.

Tell them that the new scene can be serious or light-hearted, and not to worry if they do not know how to end it. It can be very frustrating and time-consuming to try to think of a punchline to end the sketch. Bring the groups back together and ask for volunteers to act out what happened next. It works very well if more than one team act out the results.

5.2 Last day at school

Level   Elementary +

Time   15–20 minutes

Aims   To predict missing words. To improvise a sketch with some missing information.

Preparation

Photocopy Sketch 2 on page 109. To prepare for the activity below, tippex out the underlined words.

Procedure

1   Put the students in pairs and give them a copy of the script with some key words deleted. As you will see, it is easy to predict the kind of words which are missing. However, if you think some of the students will need some help with this, you can discuss it as a plenary activity, before the students divide into pairs.

2   Ask students to try to complete the sketch using their own words. Then invite volunteers to act out the sketch in front of the rest of the class.

Follow-up

Discussion. The end of the sketch indicates that the pupil thinks that he or she has connections in the right places and therefore doesn't need qualifications to get a good job. Is this a realistic possibility in your country? If it is, is it a bad thing?

Read the *Follow-up* about predicting what happens next at the end of Activity 5.1.

5.3 School friends

Level   Pre-intermediate +

Time   15 minutes

Aims   To devise a sketch with some personal information.

Preparation

The *School friends* sketch requires students to imagine that they are old school friends meeting after a number of years. Photocopy Sketch 3 on page 110. There are gaps which will require students to provide some real information about themselves and the place they are from, and also some invented information. If the students in the group are all in the same state school or college, the first details will be the same, but after that they will diversify.

Procedure

1 Put the students in pairs and ask them to read the sketch. Where there are gaps, there is an indication of what is missing, from *(name)* to *(famous acting school)*. When the students fill the gaps, some information will of course be the same, but not all, so the dialogues that they devise will not be identical to all the others in the class/group.

2 Ask the students to complete all the missing information and then rehearse the sketch.

3 Ask for volunteers to act out the sketch. It can be very entertaining for the class to watch more than one version.

Follow-up

Discussion: ask the class what it would be like to meet a classmate by chance after a few years. What kind of things would you notice? What questions would you ask? If it turned out that the other person was very successful in his/her work, would you be pleased or envious?

Read Activity 5.1 *Follow-up* about predicting what happens next.

5.4 Bert and the bulldozer

Level Pre-intermediate +

Time 15–30 minutes

Aims To predict content from a few key lines.

Preparation

Photocopy Sketch 4 on p 111, but do not distribute the photocopies until you have had the discussion outlined in the procedure below. The team leader needs to read the notes in the procedure so that he/she knows what information to 'feed' to the group.

Procedure

1 This activity requires the class to think about the possible scenarios that a given list of lines from the sketch could refer to. The team leader, having read the sketch, describes the situation little by little, revealing key lines one by one. Note that you can give narrative information in the present tense. The situation can be described as follows:

A man knocks on the front door of a house. When a woman answers the door, he says: 'Good morning. Are you ready to leave?' Who do you think the man is? What does the question suggest is about to happen?

At this early stage, the students can offer suggestions like *Taxi driver. The woman has ordered a taxi.* The team leader continues with the narrative:

However, the woman is surprised, because she isn't expecting to leave the house. When she indicates that she doesn't understand what he wants, he replies: 'Are you ready to move out of your house?'

Ask the students if this line means something different from *Are you ready to leave?* They may think that it's more final, so now they will probably think the man is a removal person. But the woman is still surprised. What do you think is happening? The team leader continues with the narrative:

The man then explains: 'We're going to knock your house down.' The woman is shocked when she hears this.

Why do you think the man wants to knock the house down? And why doesn't the woman know about this? Continue with the story:

This is the man's next line: Didn't you get the letter from the Ministry of Transport?

Now it may be clearer and you can predict more of the content. Do you think any other characters will appear in this sketch? And what do you think will happen?

2   When the class have run out of ideas, give them photocopies of the sketch. You can put them in groups, or let them read it as a whole class.

3   This is one of the sketches where the less proficient students can do something which helps them feel useful in the group. After reading and casting it, ask some of the non-speaking characters to work out how to mime a bulldozer. A traditional bulldozer has caterpillar tracks. These are used instead of wheels on vehicles such as construction equipment and tanks, which allow the vehicles to distribute their weight more evenly. If there are athletic students in the class, they may want to do forward rolls to indicate the movement of the bulldozer.

4   And of course there is Bert, whose name appears in the title of the sketch, but who does not have a speaking part. Once the students have devised how to represent the bulldozer, Bert has to sit on top of it. Students can also represent the walls of the house, which are knocked down at the end of the piece.

Variation

You can if you wish ask students to devise a sketch based on the key lines that you tell them. This may result in some very different interpretations, especially if you do not tell them the line about the Ministry of Transport.

Follow-up

Discussion: there are two serious issues which are raised in this sketch:

- the increase in the number of motorways, which is the direct result of the increase in the number of vehicles on the road
- the fact that these motorways often destroy communities. Is this something that happens in your country? Are people compensated well for losing their homes? What do the students feel about it?

Encourage students to rewrite the sketch, using a motorway building project from your area as the back-drop. Read Activity 5.1 *Follow-up* about predicting what happens next.

5.5 The old days

Level Pre-intermediate +

Time 15–20 minutes

Aims To re-order lines in the middle of a sketch.

Preparation

If you want to do the jumbled lines activity, photocopy the worksheet version of Sketch 5 on page 113. You can either cut the lines in italics into strips for students to rearrange, or use the tick-boxes to number the lines in the correct order. If you just want to rehearse and perform the sketch, photocopy the complete version on page 112.

Procedure

1 Put the class in pairs and ask them to read the beginning and the end of the sketch, and then go back to try to put the lines in *italics* in the correct order. There is only one way to complete the task. You can if you wish ask the students to do it by themselves first.

2 Whether they attempt the task by themselves or in pairs, it's good to let them help each other when they have finished. Allow the students to mingle and check each other's answers. This way, they will do a lot of reading, and they will be reading the same thing over and over again.

3 If you decide you want to act the sketch out, give the class time to think about how to act the part of an older person. You can do this as a whole-group activity. Ask them to practise talking and moving like an old person. You can have an 'old person competition', to see who can talk and move most convincingly.

The jumbled lines activity is a good one to use as a classroom reading task, so if you prefer, you can ask the class to do the activity alone and you can mark it.

Variation

If you live in an area where there has been a lot of change, ask the class to rewrite the sketch, using real places near you which have changed.

Follow-up

Read Activity 5.1 *Follow-up* about predicting what happens next.

5.6 Welcome to Mexico!

Level Intermediate +

Time 15–20 minutes

Aims To connect two parts of a sketch by improvising the missing section.

Preparation

If you want to do the improvisation activity, photocopy the worksheet version of Sketch 6 on pages 115–6. If you just want to rehearse and perform the sketch, photocopy the complete version on page 114.

Procedure

1 You can if you wish begin with a similar activity to the one in Activity 5.4. Write the following exchange on the board:

Good afternoon, sir. Welcome to Mexico City!
Pardon?
Welcome to Mexico City!
Mexico City?
Yes.
Isn't this Hong Kong?

2 Ask the students to read the lines and discuss who is speaking, and how this conversation could possibly take place. This discussion can be whole class or in groups.

3 The worksheet idea is that the students should read the first and last parts of the sketch, and then improvise a scene which connects them. You can divide the students into pairs or groups. If they are in pairs, they can all devise a scene and then some of the pairs act out the whole sketch. However, it may be better to have more people working together in a group, so they can pool their ideas. If there are three or four groups doing this, they can then cast the sketch from within the group.

Follow-up

Read Activity 5.1 *Follow-up* about predicting what happens next.

In this case, it might be interesting to act out 'What happened first?' The passenger is holding a ticket in the name of Entwistle, but claims his name is Bradshaw. If we assume that his version of events is true, students can try to act out what happened in the departure lounge before the plane left London.

Comments

This activity is set at Intermediate + as it requires more language and improvisation skills than earlier sketches.

5.7 Arachnophobia

Level Pre-intermediate +

Time 15–30 minutes

Aims To complete a sketch by finding the right place for one character's lines.

Preparation

Photocopy Sketch 7 on page 118–9. One character's lines are filled in, and the other character's lines are in a separate list. You can either cut the lines in *italics* into strips for students to rearrange, or use the tick-boxes to number the lines in the correct order. If you prefer to rehearse and perform the complete sketch, photocopy the complete version on page 117.

It helps with the performance of this sketch if both characters are holding cardboard boxes.

Procedure

1 Put the class into pairs, and ask them to work out the order of the lines in *italics*. It is fairly easy to work it out. Ask a pair to stand up and act out what they think the finished version is. It really doesn't matter if they have come up with an alternative order for the lines, although it is unlikely that they will with this sketch, which has been carefully written to avoid this happening.

2 If you prefer, you can do this as a whole-class activity. This way, the stronger students help the weaker ones.

Follow up

Ask the students to work in pairs and rewrite the sketch, using two different things that they could be frightened of. Ask them to rehearse it and act it out for the rest of the class. If the students work in small groups, they can help each other with ideas, and then they can cast it themselves, deciding who should play the sketch in front of the rest of the class. Advise them to head towards the same punchline as the original.

Read Activity 5.1 *Follow-up* about predicting what happens next.

Comment

In case your students do not understand the meaning of the title, it means 'fear of spiders'. You could take the opportunity to check on other phobias—claustrophobia, agoraphbia, etc. Fear of snakes is ophidiophobia.

5.8 The restaurant

Level   Intermediate +

Time   15 minutes

Aims   To interpret a sketch in different ways.

Preparation

The sketch is a conversation between a waiter (or waitress) and a customer in a restaurant. There are three versions of the sketch. In the first version, the waiter is polite and the customer is quite rude. In the second, the customer is more polite, but the waiter is rude. In the third version, they are both rude. To get the best value out of this activity, it is important that the characters keep more or less to the written lines and do not improvise different attitudes or emotions. It works best if three different groups work on a version each, and rehearse it where the others cannot hear them.

The sketches should be performed in the order in which they appear in this book: Version 1, 2, and finally 3.

Procedure

1   Divide the class into three groups. Photocopy each version of Sketch 8 on pages 120–2 and give each group one version of the sketch. Ask them to go away and read it through and cast it. The team leader should visit each group to see how they are getting on. Try to make sure that they are blocking the sketch the same way, in other words that the customer is sitting at the table the same way, the waiter enters from the same side and stands at the same side of the table when he/she speaks.

2   Bring the groups back together again and ask the cast who have been rehearsing the first version to act it out. When they have finished, ask the second cast to act out the scene. Finally, the third group act out Version 3.

Follow-up

At the end of the performance of the three versions, discuss what you saw. If the emotions were not clearly different, try to work out why. Who was not rude enough? Or who was not polite?

Read the *Follow-up* about predicting what happens next at the end of Activity 5.1.

Comments

Again, this sketch is flagged as Intermediate + because of the work the students need to do on interpretation.

Sketch 1
Noisy neighbours

Scene 1

Helen: Oh no! It's started again!

Michael: What?

Helen: The music!

Michael: Music? What music?

Helen: Next door! Can't you hear the music they're playing?

Michael: Yes. But it's not too bad.

Helen: Not too bad? It's deafening!

Michael: Oh come on! You're exaggerating.

Helen: I'm NOT exaggerating! I can't hear myself think!

Michael: Well what are you going to do about it?

Helen: WE are going to complain.

Michael: We? Leave me out of this. I haven't got a problem with it.

Helen: All right. I'll go and talk to them myself!

Scene 2. Knocking at door; door opens.

Woman: Hi! Come in!

Helen: Er … pardon?

Woman: Come in! Are you a friend of Eric's?

Helen: No. I live next door.

Woman: Oh! Nice to meet you! Come in!

Helen: Actually, I've come to complain about the music.

Woman: Pardon?

Helen: I'VE COME TO COMPLAIN ABOUT THE MUSIC!

Woman: Is it too loud? We can turn it down!

Helen: Thank you.

Woman: But why don't you come in anyway?

Helen: Er … OK, thank you!

Scene 3. Two hours later.

Michael: Where have you been? It's nearly midnight!

Helen: I've been at the party next door.

Michael: But you've been there for two hours!

Helen: If you were worried, why didn't you come and get me?

Michael: I did! I knocked on the door for about ten minutes but no one came to the door. The music was even louder than when you went to complain!!

Helen: Really? I didn't notice. I was dancing.

Michael: I started to shout through the window. TURN THE MUSIC DOWN! I CAN'T HEAR MYSELF THINK!

Helen: And what happened?

Michael: A police officer came along and told me to leave or he would have to arrest me.

Helen: Arrest you? Why?

Michael: Because I was making too much noise!

Sketch 2
Last day at school

There is a knock at the door.

Head: Come in?
Pupil: Good morning, head teacher.
Head: Ah, Smith. Come in.
Pupil: My name isn't Smith, head teacher, it's Jones.
Head: Yes, yes, of course, Jones. Sit down. Now, Jones, today is your last day at school. Tomorrow is the first day of the rest of your life. What do you want to do with it?
Pupil: With what?
Head: Your life, Jones, your life! What is your ambition?
Pupil: I want to be a television newsreader.
Head: A television newsreader? Why do you want to do that?
Pupil: Because television newsreaders earn a lot of money, head teacher.
Head: That's true.
Pupil: And they meet lots of interesting people.
Head: Yes, yes, but Jones, if you want to be a television newsreader, you have to study politics and economics.
Pupil: That's right.
Head: Have you studied politics and economics?
Pupil: No, head teacher.
Head: What subjects HAVE you studied?
Pupil: Art, chemistry, and geography.
Head: Art, chemistry, and geography?
Pupil: Yes.
Head: In that case, you can't possibly be a television newsreader.
Pupil: Yes, I can.
Head: How?
Pupil: My uncle is the managing director of a television news company.
Head: Oh. I see.

Sketch 3
School friends

A: Excuse me?
B: Yes?
A: Are you (*name*)?
B: Yes, I am.
A: Hi! How are you?
B: Sorry ... do we know each other?
A: Yes! I'm (*name*).
B: Have we met before?
A: Yes! We were at school together!
B: Were we?
A: Yes. You went to (*school name*), didn't you?
B: Yes.
A: Well, we were in the same class.
B: Were we? Sorry, I don't remember.
A: We used to sit next to each other in the (*subject*) class.
B: Did we?
A: Don't you remember?
B: No, sorry. I wasn't really interested in (*subject*).
A: And we used to play (*sport*) together.
B: Oh yes—it was terrible!
A: Didn't you like (*sport*)?
B: No, I hated it.
A: And we used to go/go to (*social activity/place*) every Saturday night! Do you remember?
B: No, can't remember anything like that.
A: So ... what did you do when you left (*name of school*)?
B: I studied acting at the (*famous acting school*).
A: Really?
B: Yes, I'm a very successful actor now.
A: Good.
B: What about you?
A: Well, I studied literature at (*country's best university*) and now I'm a director at the National Theatre.
B: Really? Maybe you can give me a job!
A: Maybe.
B: Yes! Now I remember you! I remember sitting next to you in (*subject*) and playing (*sport*) and going/going to (*social activity/place*)!
A: Do you?
B: Yes! And yes, I remember you now. We were best friends!
A: Were we? You know, suddenly, I can't remember you at all.

Sketch 4
Bert and the bulldozer

A workman knocks at the door of a house.

Workman:	Good morning, madam.
Woman:	Good morning.
Workman:	Are you ready to leave?
Woman:	I beg your pardon?
Workman:	Are you ready to leave? Are you ready to move out of your house?
Woman:	What are you talking about?
Workman:	Well, we're going to knock your house down.
Woman:	What?
Workman:	Yes, madam! Didn't you get the letter from the Ministry of Transport?
Woman:	What letter?
Workman:	The letter telling you about the demolition.
Woman:	No, I didn't!
Workman:	What a pity. Well, I'm sorry, but we have to knock your house down. Bert! Bring the bulldozer!

There is the sound of a bulldozer starting up.

Woman:	Stop! Henry! HENRY!
Man:	Hello?
Woman:	Come here quickly!
Man:	What's going on?
Woman:	This man has just told me that he's going to knock the house down.
Man:	Oh. What?
Workman:	Didn't you get the letter from the Ministry of Transport?
Man/Woman:	No!
Workman:	Ah well, if I were you, I'd call them about it.
Man:	Why do you want to knock our house down?
Workman:	Because your house is directly in the path of the new motorway!
Man:	What new motorway?
Workman:	The … er … M111352 from … I don't know … from somewhere to somewhere … via your house, I'm afraid!
Woman:	You are NOT going to knock down our house!
Man:	Yes. Go and knock down someone else's house!
Workman:	I'm sorry. Our orders are quite clear. We have to knock down numbers 41, 42, 43, 44, and 45 Railway Street.
Woman:	This is number 46.
Workman:	What?
Man:	This isn't number 41, 42, 43, 44, or 45. This is number 46.
Workman:	Is it? Oh, well that's all right then. Sorry to have troubled you! Bert! It's the wrong house. Bert! Stop! Beeeeeeeeeeeeert!!!

There is the sound of a house being demolished.

Workman:	Oh dear …

Sketch 5
The old days

A young person meets an old person in the centre of a village.

Young person:	Good morning!
Old person:	Good morning.
Young person:	Nice day, isn't it?
Old person:	It's all right.
Young person:	This is a lovely village.
Old person:	Do you think so?
Young person:	Yes, I do. It's beautiful.
Old person:	It used to be beautiful. Not any more.
Young person:	Have you lived here long?
Old person:	All my life.
Young person:	Aha. You must have seen some changes.
Old person:	Yes, I have. Do you see those houses over there?
Young person:	Yes. They look very nice.
Old person:	That used to be fields. You could see all the way to the river. Not any more.
Young person:	No. But they ARE very nice houses.
Old person:	I suppose so, if you like that sort of thing.
Young person:	Well, people have to live somewhere.
Old person:	And do you see that hotel over there? That used to be a railway station.
Young person:	Really? Why did they close it?
Old person:	Because there weren't any trains.
Young person:	Oh. Well, it's a very nice hotel.
Old person:	How do you know?
Young person:	Because I'm staying there.
Old person:	And you see that Italian restaurant over there?
Young person:	Yes. It's marvellous. I went there last night. The food is superb.
Old person:	That used to be a fish and chip shop.
Young person:	Oh, I'm sorry. That's very sad for the village.
Old person:	No, it isn't. They made horrible fish and chips.
Young person:	So … it's probably better that it closed.
Old person:	Yes, I suppose so.
Young person:	Oh well, have a nice day.
Old person:	No, thank you, I've made other plans.

Sketch 5
The old days: Worksheet

A young person meets an old person in the centre of a village.

Young person:	Good morning!
Old person:	Good morning.
Young person:	Nice day, isn't it?
Old person:	It's all right.
Young person:	This is a lovely village.
Old person:	Do you think so?
Young person:	Yes, I do. It's beautiful
Old person:	It used to be beautiful. Not any more.
Young person:	Have you lived here long?
Old person:	All my life.
Young person:	Aha. You must have seen some changes.
Old person:	Yes, I have. Do you see those houses over there?

✂ -

☐ *Old person:*   *And do you see that hotel over there? That used to be a railway station.*

☐ *Old person:*   *And you see that Italian restaurant over there?*

☐ *Old person:*   *Because there weren't any trains.*

☐ *Old person:*   *How do you know?*

☐ *Old person:*   *I suppose so, if you like that sort of thing.*

☐ *Old person:*   *That used to be a fish and chip shop.*

☐ *Old person:*   *That used to be fields. You could see all the way to the river. Not any more.*

☐ *Young person:*   *Because I'm staying there.*

☐ *Young person:*   *No. But they ARE very nice houses.*

☐ *Young person:*   *Oh. Well, it's a very nice hotel.*

☐ *Young person:*   *Really? Why did they close it?*

☐ *Young person:*   *Well, people have to live somewhere.*

☐ *Young person:*   *Yes. It's marvellous. I went there last night. The food is superb.*

☐ *Young person:*   *Yes. They look very nice.*

- -

Young person:	Oh, I'm sorry. That's very sad for the village.
Old person:	No, it isn't. They made horrible fish and chips.
Young person:	So … it's probably better that it closed.
Old person:	Yes, I suppose so.
Young person:	Oh well, have a nice day.
Old person:	No, thank you, I've made other plans.

Sketch 6
Welcome to Mexico!

Immigration Officer:	Good afternoon, sir. Welcome to Mexico City!
Passenger:	Pardon?
Immigration Officer:	Welcome to Mexico City!
Passenger:	Mexico City?
Immigration Officer:	Yes.
Passenger:	Isn't this Hong Kong?
Immigration Officer:	No. This is Mexico City.
Passenger:	I'm supposed to be in Hong Kong!
Immigration Officer:	Well, I'm sorry to disappoint you, sir, but this is Mexico City International Airport.
Passenger:	Are you sure?
Immigration Officer:	Well, I've only been working here for 15 years but ... yes, of course I'm sure!
Passenger:	How is it possible?
Immigration Officer:	Well, the Aztecs built a city near here in the 14th century, and after that ...
Passenger:	No, I mean—how did I get here?
Immigration Officer:	I expect you came on that Jumbo Jet outside.
Passenger:	But I wanted to go to Hong Kong!
Immigration Officer:	Let me have a look at your ticket. No, Mr Entwistle, this is definitely a ticket to Mexico City.
Passenger:	Entwistle? My name isn't Entwistle. My name is Bradshaw!
Immigration Officer:	So ... you're in the wrong airport and you have the wrong ticket and passport. Can you explain this?
Passenger:	I don't know! I'm confused!
Immigration Officer:	Let's start at the beginning. Tell me exactly what happened to you ...
Passenger:	Well, I went to London airport and I checked in for the flight to Hong Kong.
Immigration Officer:	And then?
Passenger:	And then I went to the departure lounge.
Immigration Officer:	So far, so good.
Passenger:	Then I sat down and fell asleep. I woke up suddenly when I heard an announcement: Last call, Gate number 7 ... So I ran towards the gate.
Immigration Officer:	Yes?
Passenger:	And I ran into someone.
Immigration Officer:	Who?
Passenger:	No idea. Another passenger.
Immigration Officer:	I see.
Passenger:	We both dropped things on the floor—bags, passports—I picked my things up continued running. I showed my ticket to someone and they showed me where to go. Then I got on the plane and fell asleep. I woke up when we landed.
Immigration Officer:	Very interesting story but I don't believe a word of it.
Passenger:	But it's true! You must believe me!

Sketch 6
Welcome to Mexico! Worksheet

Immigration Officer:	Good afternoon, sir. Welcome to Mexico City!
Passenger:	Pardon?
Immigration Officer:	Welcome to Mexico City!
Passenger:	Mexico City?
Immigration Officer:	Yes.
Passenger:	Isn't this Hong Kong?
Immigration Officer:	No. This is Mexico City.
Passenger:	I'm supposed to be in Hong Kong!
Immigration Officer:	Well, I'm sorry to disappoint you, sir, but this is Mexico City International Airport.
Passenger:	Are you sure?
Immigration Officer:	Well, I've only been working here for 15 years but ... yes, of course I'm sure!
Passenger:	How is it possible?
Immigration Officer:	Well, the Aztecs built a city near here in the 14th century, and after that ...
Passenger:	No, I mean—how did I get here?
Immigration Officer:	I expect you came on that Jumbo Jet outside.
Passenger:	But I wanted to go to Hong Kong!
Immigration Officer:	Let me have a look at your ticket. No, Mr Entwistle, this is definitely a ticket to Mexico City.
Passenger:	Entwistle? My name isn't Entwistle. My name is Bradshaw!
Immigration Officer:	So....you're in the wrong airport and you have the wrong ticket and passport. Can you explain this?
Passenger:	I don't know! I'm confused!

Photocopiable © Oxford University Press

Immigration Officer:	Let's start at the beginning. Tell me exactly what happened to you …
_____	_____
_____	_____
_____	_____
_____	_____
_____	_____
_____	_____
_____	_____
_____	_____
_____	_____
_____	_____
Immigration Officer:	Very interesting story but I don't believe a word of it.
Passenger:	But it's true! You must believe me!

Sketch 7
Arachnophobia

Steve:	What have you got in that box?
Hazel:	A spider.
Steve:	A spider?! Uuuuuuuugh! I'm terrified of spiders! Kill it!
Hazel:	Kill it? No way!
Steve:	Well, throw it out of the window, then.
Hazel:	I certainly will NOT throw it out of the window!
Steve:	But it's a spider. Spiders are horrible.
Hazel:	Spiders are not horrible. They're beautiful! And my spider is especially beautiful.
Steve:	What do you mean, YOUR spider?
Hazel:	My spider. It belongs to me. His name is Henry.
Steve:	Henry???
Hazel:	Yes. Henry's from Africa. He's very rare and he's very valuable. Do you want to have a look at him?
Steve:	No, I DON'T want to have a look at him!
Hazel:	Come on, it's just a spider! Let me open the box and ...
Steve:	No! Don't open the box! Don't you understand? I'm absolutely terrified of spiders!
Hazel:	Oh you are SUCH a baby! Take a deep breath, and look in the box.
Steve:	OK ... Hmm ... yes. He's quite nice, isn't he? He's hairy and ... very nice.
Hazel:	See? So no need to be frightened, right?
Steve:	Right.
Hazel:	By the way, what have you got in YOUR box?
Steve:	Daisy.
Hazel:	Daisy?
Steve:	Yes. Daisy is my snake.
Hazel:	A snake???
Steve:	Yes. Do you want to see her?
Hazel:	Noooo! I'm terrified of snakes!
Steve:	Oh come on. Look! She's lovely!
Hazel:	Noooooooooooooo!
Steve:	You ARE funny. She's only a snake.

Sketch 7
Arachnophobia: Worksheet

Steve: What have you got in that box?

Hazel: _____

Steve: A spider?!? Uuuuuuuuugh! I'm terrified of spiders! Kill it!

Hazel: _____

Steve: Well, throw it out of the window, then.

Hazel: _____

Steve: But it's a spider. Spiders are horrible.

Hazel: _____

Steve: What do you mean, YOUR spider?

Hazel: _____

Steve: Henry???

Hazel: _____

Steve: No, I DON'T want to have a look at him!

Hazel: _____

Steve: No! Don't open the box! Don't you understand? I'm absolutely terrified
of spiders!

Hazel: _____

Steve: OK … Hmm … yes. He's quite nice, isn't he? He's hairy and … very nice.

Hazel: _____

Steve: Right.

Hazel: _____

Steve: Daisy.

Hazel: _____

Steve: Yes. Daisy is my snake.

Hazel: _____

Steve: Yes. Do you want to see her?

Hazel: _____

Steve: Oh come on. Look! She's lovely!

Hazel: _____

Steve: You ARE funny. She's only a snake.

☐	Hazel:	A snake???
☐	Hazel:	A spider.
☐	Hazel:	By the way, what have you got in YOUR box?
☐	Hazel:	Come on, it's just a spider! Let me open the box and ...
☐	Hazel:	Daisy?
☐	Hazel:	I certainly will NOT throw it out of the window!
☐	Hazel:	Kill it? No way!
☐	Hazel:	My spider. It belongs to me. His name is Henry.
☐	Hazel:	Noooo! I'm terrified of snakes!
☐	Hazel:	Nooooooooooooo!
☐	Hazel:	Oh you are SUCH a baby! Take a deep breath, and look in the box.
☐	Hazel:	See? So no need to be frightened, right?
☐	Hazel:	Spiders are not horrible. They're beautiful! And my spider is especially beautiful.
☐	Hazel:	Yes. Henry's from Africa. He's very rare and he's very valuable. Do you want to have a look at him?

Sketch 8
Restaurant sketch (Version 1)

Customer:	Waiter!
Waiter:	Can I help you, sir?
Customer:	This soup.
Waiter:	The soup?
Customer:	Yes. The soup. It's cold.
Waiter:	Aha ... well, sir, it's gazpacho.
Customer:	What's gazpacho?
Waiter:	It's Spanish, sir. It's supposed to be cold.
Customer:	Well, I don't want it. Take it away.
Waiter:	Very good, sir.
Customer:	Oh, and waiter!
Waiter:	Yes, sir?
Customer:	This bread.
Waiter:	The bread?
Customer:	Yes. The bread. It's too hard.
Waiter:	Well, sir, it's granary bread. You're right. It IS a bit harder than other breads.
Customer:	Well take it away and bring me some sliced white bread.
Waiter:	Very good, sir.
Customer:	And take this butter away, too!
Waiter:	Is there something wrong with the butter?
Customer:	It's also too hard. Bring me some nice soft margarine.
Waiter:	Very good, sir.
Customer:	And I want something to drink
Waiter:	Very good, sir. Would you like to see the wine list? We have some nice wines from France, Spain, Greece, and Italy.
Customer:	What about British wine?
Waiter:	I'm afraid we don't have any British wine, sir.
Customer:	In that case, bring me a cup of tea.
Waiter:	A cup of tea. Very good, sir.

Sketch 8
Restaurant sketch (Version 2)

Customer:	Er … excuse me?
Waiter:	What do you want?
Customer:	This soup …
Waiter:	What about it?
Customer:	I'm afraid it's cold.
Waiter:	Cold? Of course it's cold! It's gazpacho!
Customer:	What's gazpacho?
Waiter:	What's gazpacho? It's Spanish! It's supposed to be cold!
Customer:	Well, I'm sorry, I don't like it.
Waiter:	Well, you'll have to pay for it!
Customer:	What? Why?
Waiter:	Because you ordered it.
Customer:	But … I don't really want it.
Waiter:	Not my problem! You ordered it, you pay for it.
Customer:	Oh dear. Er … waiter?
Waiter:	What is it now?
Customer:	This bread is a bit hard.
Waiter:	Hard? Of course it's hard. It's granary bread!
Customer:	Could I possibly have some sliced white bread?
Waiter:	Sliced white bread? In a posh restaurant like this? You must be joking!
Customer:	And I'm afraid this butter is a bit hard too. Any chance of some margarine?
Waiter:	Margarine? You expect me to serve you margarine?? No chance, mate!
Customer:	Er … OK. May I see the wine list?
Waiter:	It's there in front of you. We have some nice wines from France, Spain, Greece, and Italy.
Customer:	What about British wine?
Waiter:	We don't sell British wine.
Customer:	In that case, bring me a cup of tea.
Waiter:	A cup of tea? I don't believe it!

Sketch 8
Restaurant sketch (Version 3)

Customer:	Waiter!
Waiter:	What do you want?
Customer:	This soup.
Waiter:	What about it?
Customer:	It's cold.
Waiter:	Cold? Of course it's cold! It's gazpacho.
Customer:	What's gazpacho?
Waiter:	What's gazpacho? It's Spanish! It's supposed to be cold!
Customer:	Well, I don't want it. Take it away.
Waiter:	Well, you'll have to pay for it!
Customer:	Pay for it? Why?
Waiter:	Because you ordered it.
Customer:	But I don't want it.
Waiter:	Not my problem! You ordered it, you pay for it.
Customer:	Waiter!
Waiter:	What is it now?
Customer:	This bread is hard.
Waiter:	Hard? Of course it's hard. It's granary bread!
Customer:	Well take it away and bring me some sliced white bread.
Waiter:	Sliced white bread? In a posh restaurant like this? You must be joking!
Customer:	And take this butter away, too! It's also too hard. Bring me some nice soft margarine.
Waiter:	Margarine? You expect me to serve you margarine? No chance, mate!
Customer:	And I want something to drink.
Waiter:	The wine list is in front of you. We have some nice wines from France, Spain, Greece, and Italy.
Customer:	What about British wine?
Waiter:	We don't sell British wine, sir.
Customer:	In that case, bring me a cup of tea.
Waiter:	A cup of tea? I don't believe it!

Further reading

Books written specifically for ELT

Case, Doug and Wilson, Ken. 1995. *English Sketches 1 and 2*. Oxford: Macmillan.

Hadfield, Jill. 1992. *Classroom Dynamics*. Oxford: Oxford University Press.

Klippel, Friederike. 1984. *Keep Talking*. Cambridge: Cambridge University Press.

Maley, Alan and Duff, Alan. 2005. *Drama Techniques in Language Learning*. 3rd edition. Cambridge: Cambridge University Press.

Ur, Penny and Wright, Andrew. 1992. *Five-Minute activities*. Cambridge: Cambridge University Press.

Watcyn-Jones, Peter. 1978. *Act English*. London: Penguin.

Books on drama and drama teaching

Abbott, John. 2008. *The Improvisation Book – How to Conduct Successful Improvisation Sessions*. London: Nick Hern Books.

Barker, Clive. 1977. *Theatre Games*. London: A & C Black.

Deary, Terence. 1977. *Teaching Through Theatre*. London: Samuel French.

Fleming, Michael. 1997. *The Art of Drama Teaching*. London: David Fulton Publishers.

Graham, Ginny. 1993. *First Stage: A Drama Handbook for Schools and Youth Theatres.* Tavistock: Northcote House Publishers.

Heathcote, Dorothy and Bolton, Gavin. 1995. *Drama for Learning: Dorothy Heathcote's Mantle of the Expert Approach to Education*. Portsmouth, NH: Heinemann.

Johnstone, Keith. 1981. *Impro: Improvisation and the Theatre*. London: A & C Black.

Johnstone, Keith. 1999. *Impro for Storytellers*. London: Faber and Faber.

Lewis, Martin and Rainer, John. 2005. *Teaching Classroom Drama and Theatre*. London: Routledge.

Polsky, Milton. 1989. *Let's Improvise – Becoming Creative, Expressive and Spontaneous Through Drama*. Maryland: University Press of America.

Scher, Anna and Verrall, Charles. 1975. *100+ Ideas for Drama*. London: Heinemann.

Scher, Anna and Verrall, Charles. 1987. *Another 100+ Ideas for Drama*. London: Heinemann.

Spolin, Viola. 1963. *Improvisation for the Theater*. Chicago: Northwestern University Press.

Spolin, Viola. 1985. *Theater Games for Rehearsal*. Chicago: Northwestern University Press.

Spolin, Viola. 1986. *Theater Games for the Classroom*. Chicago: Northwestern University Press.

Wagner, Betty Jane. 1979. *Dorothy Heathcote: Drama as a Learning Medium*. London: Hutchinson.

Website

There are hundreds of activities at this website. http://improvencyclopedia.org

Index